Diversity, Inclusion & Belonging

A Leadership Guide About Why Everyone Matters and How to Make Everyone Feel Like They Do

By Leila McKenzie Delis

Illustrated By Richard Deverell

D0863065

PublishNation
www.publishnation.co.uk

Dedication

This book is dedicated to my wonderful family – my Mum, Anne, Dad, Rod and brother Mikey. You inspire me to work hard and to be myself. To my husband and love of my life, Costa, you make me believe that anything is possible. To the people out there in the world trying to make a difference and striving for positive change. To my inner sanctum and team at DIAL Global. You all inspire me everyday. x

Contents

CHAPTER-BY-CHAPTER SUMMARY

Foreword

*"The book **"Diversity, Inclusion and Belonging"** by Leila McKenzie Delis resonates very much with my personal experience and life journey, having spent more than 20 years at Starbucks and a number of years at PizzaExpress. Since the very beginning, Starbucks Mission and Values have reflected its fundamental principle that "we welcome everyone", which fosters and builds a diverse, inclusive and equitable work culture of innovation, new ideas, development, growth and business success around the world. One of the core values at PizzaExpress is the family inclusiveness with a diverse workforce with more than 100 nationalities – serving diverse communities and places for people and family gathering and connection. We deliver value and sustainable business success by living our values. Humanity is universe and tolerance is virtue.*

- *__Diversity__ is not simply limited to race, gender or ethnicity, but also to the power of differences in mindset and approach and goes as wide as considering other elements such as belief, culture, social mobility, experience and thought.*
- *__Inclusivity__ in every sense of the word is a business imperative for any organisation of the future looking to both thrive and sustain profitability.*
- *__Belonging__ is one of the most important seeing values in life and being accepted totally for who you are and what you stand for.*
- *__Community__ beyond one's family, workplace and community is where we spend the majority of our time*

and life. Instead of individuals being concerned about their differences we should be embracing these unique traits in order to harness the good that humankind has to offer.

We find ourselves living in an uncertain, complex, and ambiguous world today and so it is more important now than ever before to create places that are safe for people to be themselves and bring their full selves to the table, both personally and professionally. We must seek to cast the net as widely as possible in order to harness the power of different people, cultures and experiences from around the world.

I met Leila when she wrote to me and then visited my office in London a couple of years ago. She has remained in contact since and I have been pleased to see the work she has achieved moving the dial in the right direction for diversity, inclusion and belonging.

Leila is a strong example of a Millennial thought-leader today trying to embrace the benefits of change in the complex world we live in. Her book is a testament to the leaders in the world striving for better and also gives some strong tools and practical examples that can be utilised by others wanting to make positive change happen and create a better world for us all."

Jinlong Wang, Group CEO and Chairman, Pizza Express Group Managing Director and Operating Partner, Hony Capital

Praise for Leila McKenzie Delis
& Diversity, Inclusion & Belonging

"If you want to be a force for change, and you don't know where to start... start here."
Leena Nair, Chief Human Resources Officer, Unilever

"This book on diversity, inclusion and belongingness is a game changer. It shows just how important this topic is to business—get it, you won't be disappointed."
Professor Sir Cary Cooper, CBE, 50th Anniversary Professor of Organizational Psychology & Health, Alliance Manchester Business School

"Leila is an exceptionally talented young woman and her personal story is a powerful and thought-provoking message as to why successful leaders champion diversity, inclusion and belonging. She delivers a simple and compelling lesson to all leaders – that to succeed, 'business as usual' will have to incorporate 'business as unusual'. An inspiring read."
Debbie Hewitt, MBE, Chairman, Visa Europe, Non Executive Chairman, Moss Bros Group plc, The Restaurant Group plc, BGL (owners of comparethemarket.com) & Wright Stuff.

'Cover to cover an engaging and inspirational read – for leaders who belong to tomorrow'
Kari Daniels, Chief Executive Officer, Tesco Ireland

"Invaluable. An excellent contribution, to an important debate."
Clive Myrie, Journalist, News Presenter and World Affairs Correspondent

"A great book for anyone wanting to achieve Belonging in their workplace through embarking on a journey of true inclusion in an authentic way, that no doubt will have long lasting benefits for both individuals and the organisation itself"
Asif Sadiq MBE, Head of Diversity, Inclusion and Belonging, Telegraph Media Group.

"Creating workplaces that are grounded in belonging and bravery requires leaders that are truly committed to the growth and development of humans - and this book explores and shares the steps and process needed to create this much-needed transformation today."
Claude Silver, Chief Heart Officer, VaynerMedia

"There cannot be a more diverse community than the one that includes so many different cultures as Britain does, providing the most conducive environment for everyone to achieve their full potential. I may have not come across a better book on diversity and inclusion than this piece of work by Leila. A real thought-provoking book, seriously!"
Rohit Shelatkar, Director, Vitabiotics Ltd. CEO, Vision World, Founder and CEO, Grand Maratha Foundation

"Leila McKenzie Delis is a leading authority on diversity and inclusion, supporting senior leaders from successful global and local organisations achieve higher performing results, including purpose and profit. This book will inspire you and help you believe you can make a real difference and a sense of belonging. A compelling read!"
Campbell Fitch, Chief People Officer and Governor, Glasgow Caledonian University

"The energy of people is the most important asset to organisations in this very VUCA world. This book provides a wonderful insight into how being able to be truly yourself and bring your whole self to work, contributes to that asset, and therefore the performance of an organisation irrespective of it size and scope of work"
Geoff McDonald, Co-Founder Minds at Work, Former VPHR Unilever

"Leila McKenzie Delis is different; her book is different. When you thought you knew all you needed to know about Diversity, along comes Leila to remind us all about the importance of belonging and the role of the leader in truly doing more.
Her personal story is compelling and her words inspire us all to listen, to hear and to truly take action to make a difference.
Feelings, purpose and authenticity are important ingredients in bringing diversity to life and Leila makes sure we know the 'what', the 'why' and the 'how'.
She makes it real, she keeps it simple. She makes us think. And she makes us act."
Leann Hearne, Group CEO, First Ark

"Every success that I have enjoyed was due to the people I had the joy to empower. I work with more diverse backgrounds in the GCC than I have ever done in my 30 year career. I believe that no matter where you're from that you can all make a huge difference, but only if you respect and listen to everyone. It does not matter to me whether you're an executive or the dishwasher.
We all have a part to play in being the best we can in life and business. This book is a testament to embracing a diverse array of voices and the importance of inclusive behaviour."
Ian John Toal, CEO, Alfaco

"Much is said about diversity, inclusion and the changing environment in which employees are looking for other reasons to be part of a network, team or organisation than just a salary. To create a habitat in which all individuals have a feeling of belonging and, as a collabaration, are able to cope with today's challenges, Leila McKenzie Delis has written a practical guide providing leaders with both the theoretical concepts as well as various case studies that could help them in steering their organisation in our ever faster altering world.
"Diversity, Inclusion and Belonging" is a very welcome addition to the existing seminars, articles and books on the topic as it presents the reader with a consise overview on what is currently relevant."
Dr. Anthony (Ton) Martin Christiaanse MBA, Edinburgh, Chairman, AK Stoddart, Group CEO Aviko, Advisor/Investor to Private Equity and start ups

"Leading our lives with purpose is a unique gift we can all give ourselves. Be clear, be passionate and trust your journey. I have been very fortunate to meet my business partner, Leila, through our passion for inclusion and diversity and through this we are leading and living with purpose to change the world for a better place."
Minaxi Mistry, Chief Operating Officer, DIAL GLOBAL

"Exploring the essential topic of inclusion and diversity needed a thought leader, and now we have one in Leila. We needed to have someone who knows how important it is from the very core of who they are and is dynamic enough to champion it in an inspiring and heartfelt way so we can all connect with it too. Her story, ideas and passion shine out of each chapter compelling the reader to delve deep into leadership, emotional intelligence, purpose and mentoring with case studies that demystify motivation, Millennials and growth. Leila has assembled a power-packed book that gives us accessibility to cultural change, which starts from within. To see the future of Diversity and Inclusion, read Leila's genuine and masterful words."
Alexandra Watson, Editor-in-Chief SHINE UK Magazine, best-selling author, speaker, expert on female leadership and success.

"Leila is a passionate advocate of inclusivity and this insight is a real chance to walk in the shoes of someone who has experienced the stresses of surrendering a part of their true self in order to be accepted. Leila has been able to develop and grow significant understanding by working with global

enterprises to encourage cultures where everyone can contribute and feel truly valued for their skills, but also to be the person that they truly are, regardless of their own background and personal journey. As managers developing an open and accepting mindset, this should be a mandatory part of our development. This book is an important reminder of 'why'" with some great ideas on 'how!'"

David Hurren, CEO Air Liquide Advanced Business & Technologies UK

"Leila's passion for this agenda is compelling, infectious and unyielding. I suspect that this is in part because her experience of the issues she addresses is not simply theoretical, but instead real and lived. The power of this authentic experience seeps through every page of this book and it is this power that acts as clarion call to arms for all! This book is necessary. This book is prescient. This book is a must read for anyone leading in the 21st Century."

Sharon Amesu, Chair, Institute of Directors North West Region, Award-winning leadership speaker

"It only took a bit of dipping into Leila's manuscript to see if I could help her with some illustrations and I said to myself, "Wow! This is a very important book!" I hope it gets a very wide reading in the business community by leaders and aspiring leaders, as well as anyone who feels they or their colleagues or friends are struggling to belong."

Richard Deverell, Illustrator

Introduction

To feel connected, humans need to feel seen, to feel heard and to feel valued. Conversely, when our voices aren't heard, our whole selves aren't seen and our ideas aren't valued, we feel disconnected. We feel disengaged. We feel like we don't belong.

And belonging, as we'll explore in this book, is a vital motivational factor. Belonging is at the very core of our existence as human beings; it's part of our reason for being.

Every single human being – regardless of ethnicity, gender, sexuality – needs to feel they belong in order to optimally function, both in life and at work. And to feel they belong, they need to be seen, heard and valued. That's just the way it is.

"Belonging goes to the very heart of our existence as human beings. From the far reaches of our unconscious, we feel insecure if we do not belong"
Anthony Seldon

Of course, in order to be heard; those we work for and with need to listen.

So, leaders who listen, lead well.

When leaders listen, people feel included. And there are plenty of other ways leaders can foster a culture of inclusion in their workforces too.

This book is about listening leaders and the array of voices they can and should listen to. It's about honouring those different voices and cultivating a capacity to empower each valuable one. As such, *Diversity, Inclusion and Belonging* is a business book, but it's also a people book. For it explores what people and organisations alike really need in order to thrive.

Because, just as individuals have their own needs, so too do organisations.

There are many reasons why people set up their own businesses and why corporations exist – from making money and keeping the wolf from the door to financing dream lifestyles and making a difference in the world.

Whether the 'why' for the business is purpose or profit or, as is increasingly the norm, a bit of both, all business leaders share a basic need - they want the people they lead to perform at the best of their ability, to innovate and communicate well; to optimally function.

However, staff are unlikely to bring their best selves to the workplace if the very basic human need of belonging goes unmet.

The Right Kind of Workforce

Fundamentally, staff's inability to bring their true selves to work equates to a sub-optimal workforce.

Workforces shouldn't be forced to be someone they're not, just to fit in. They should become a formidable force through continual encouragement to be all that they are; to be their unique authentic selves.

When that happens, their strengths become visible and valuable.

For when we enable our talent to play to their strengths by being themselves, our enterprises are empowered.

Why then do so many business leaders fail to enable their people to bring their best and whole selves to work? That is one of the questions this book seeks to answer.

As a British Chinese millennial business leader myself, for many years I didn't bring my whole self to life, let alone to work! In order to fit in and belong, I felt a necessity to keep part of my true self hidden; to show up as people expected me to show up, rather than as the real me.

When I moved to Harrogate aged six, most of my middle-class peers hadn't ever seen a Chinese child before. That was incredibly difficult and the teasing about my eyes made me feel shy, uncomfortable, depressed and nervous.

Consequently, all I wanted was to be blond-haired and blue-eyed, so I could fit in. To belong, I just wanted to be like everyone else. I hated being different, because it was my difference, I felt, which led to being excluded rather than included.

I didn't realise being different was a strength; I saw my difference as a huge weakness and I'd do anything to try to fit in. That's what intrinsically made me unhappy and led to my anxiety and depression – feeling disempowered and unable to be myself.

I lived most of my life as a chameleon, trying to adapt and fit in to my surroundings, and not being myself. And that lack of authenticity broke me down. I didn't know what I should be, who I should follow, what I should do or how I should show-up. So I pandered to expectations, tried to fit in and only brought part of myself to the table.

Other than my wonderful parents, there were never any role models in the public eye, in business or in the media I could look up to; nobody who looked or sounded like me anyway. So I felt disconnected and disengaged. I couldn't bring my whole self to work because I felt I had to suppress it in order to belong.

And yet I can see now that I had so much potential, just like you have and just like all the people you work with, employ now or will employ in the future.

Fortunately, I've learned to bring my whole self to work and I want you to do so too – whether you're a leader now, or someone who aspires to lead one day, I not only want you to bring your whole self to work, but for you to encourage and enable others to do so.

Because I honestly believe that anyone can be a leader. The old-fashioned elitism of inaccessible hierarchies seems no longer relevant. Leadership is no longer reserved for the few. To me, leadership is about influence and inspiring positive behaviour to create change and produce meaningful results. As such, in essence, all a leader really needs is to have the ability to build a loyal following and the will to make a positive difference.

It took me a long time to see my difference as a strength. And, even when I did, it still felt difficult to show up fully. As a relatively young British Chinese girl, walking in to a room of mostly C-Suite level middle-aged white guys wasn't easy*. Especially when you often feel eyes beginning to roll backwards when you mention the D-word (Diversity).

Disclaimer: No disrespect to all the middle-aged white men out there. Aside from marrying an incredible one, many are friends and some of those admirable business leaders in positions of power who can massively effect change, are included in this book. And it's crucial for us to respect those who fit the stereotype and those who don't equally.

Thankfully, I'm incredibly enthusiastic and I've become increasingly bold as I've noticed that my genuine enthusiasm for wanting to foster positive change has on-boarded even the most stalwart executive, and has, according to them, even taught them a thing or two. After all, you don't have long to capture a busy CEO's attention when you finally get in front of them.

Whereas once I would stifle and curb my enthusiasm, these days I choose to really play on that. It's what gets me through the doors, up on stage and enables me to capture hearts and minds, because I'm passionate about my 'why' and I've started playing to my strengths and calling time on the inequality I see around me.

Imagine the impact if every single person brought their full authentic selves to work; if the entire workforce felt included, engaged, and connected. What a difference that would make to the bottom line and to achieving the purposeful goals of the company. What a powerful force of people that organisation would have.

Today, through sharing my own diversity story and incorporating it into my own leadership style, I want to help people to find their voices, embrace their authentic selves and realise that it's actually okay to be different and to bring a different perspective to their place of work. I want to bring anyone that feels like an 'outsider' in, whilst encouraging us to be true to ourselves.

It's alright not to think the same as everybody else. In fact, it's better NOT to. Group-think is not beneficial in business.

I also aim to foster business cultures which hear all those voices available to them; to enable people to bring their whole authentic selves to the workplace. That is my why...

Because everyone has a voice.

Everyone has the power to make a positive difference to the organisations in which they work; and that power should be enabled and celebrated rather than disabled and hidden.

This is the message I gave recently at an Institute of Directors talk to 50 Afro-Caribbean students who were considering their future careers, and it's the primary message of this book – for leaders to do all they can every day to make sure every single individual's voice is heard, even the unusual suspects. *Especially* the unusual suspects!

I've written this book because I want to shine a light on some of those unusual suspects – those different types of leaders, who don't fit the stereotype, but are showing up as their whole selves and getting their voices heard.

I believe business as usual should incorporate business as *unusual* in order to change and grow and stand out competitively.

Because competitive advantage is what every organisation strives for, and difference is good.

Difference Is Good

Think about it.

What's one of the first things you learn at business school?

To be sufficiently different so that you may stand out from the crowd; to have a USP (Unique Selling Point) that will give you a competitive advantage. In this way, difference and uniqueness are celebrated and cultivated. Yet, when it comes to C-suites and boards and teams, corporations seem indifferent to difference.

We continue to furnish our boards and C-suites with people who may differ in skill-sets yet are remarkably similar culturally and ethically. Grey hair and white skin populates, despite the rise in D&I initiatives over the past three decades.

- Only 2% of director positions are held by people from ethnic minorities who are UK citizens (Sir John Parker Review, July 2017).

- In fact, there are more chief executives called 'Steve' than there are from an ethnic minority in the FTSE 100. Similarly, across the pond, only three black CEOs and 11 Hispanic CEOS who head up Fortune 500 companies.

- Meanwhile, the percentage of women in leadership position on FTSE 100 boards has flatlined for a fourth year at 9.7% in 2018, with just seven female CEOs and 10 female CFOs. Meanwhile, women make up just 5 per cent of Fortune 500 CEOs, with just 24 of them female.

This is despite report upon report upon report demonstrating with utmost clarity that diverse teams perform better; that by tapping in to a broad range of different cultural backgrounds, ethnicities, genders, sexualities, across the whole spectrum of what the wonderful human race has to offer, your business will benefit.

And, not only do individual organisations benefit massively from diverse leaders and teams, so does the economy. According to a McKinsey report, eliminating the gender pay gap could add £150bn to the annual GDP by 2025, while The McGregor Review reports that the UK economy could be boosted by £24bn, contributing 1.3% growth to GDP, if BME employees advanced at the same rate as their white counterparts at work.

Yes. Difference is good – not just in terms of creating a unique product or service, but in terms of creating a unique team; one with a range of diverse voices, ideas and solutions.
The fact is, we should be nurturing originality rather than pandering to similarity. For, when we do, we have the power to propel our businesses forward and gain the ultimate competitive advantage.

Today, truly diverse and inclusive enterprises led by good leaders have an opportunity to benefit from the unique, original and authentic voices they have in their teams; they can leverage the best of their diverse teams and broaden their boards and leap ahead rather than stumble and fall.

Yet, stumble and fall they do.

From Intention to Intervention

Businesses value talent highly. They know good people are the lifeblood of their own enterprise and the entire economy. Yet still we see a lack of diverse representation.

Organisations may claim that D&I matters to their business; they might think they're being inclusive, yet they still neatly package their colleagues into groups, they segregate and silo their minority team members, thus disconnecting and disengaging their talent and preventing them from bringing their whole selves to work.

Sadly, as the statistics above prove, despite good intentions of supporting the "business case" for D&I initiatives over a number of decades, organisations have still made poor progress.

Such widespread inequality calls for an urgent requirement for leaders to change, especially because the new workforce – Millennials and Zillennials - are demanding such change, in their droves.

Consequently, leaders have a choice. They can either be reactive or proactive. Only one of these choices will enable them to gain and retain the best talent and get the most from every single one of their people.

Of course, this requires change – adaption and evolution.

Rather than mere intention we need intervention.

But it needn't be sudden. It can be gentle and incremental and still be effective.

Big steps or little steps, everyone has to start somewhere. And taking those baby steps before you crawl and then run, is critical.

On a day-to-day basis in our places of work, we need to be able to adapt to challenges and opportunities which present themselves. And it is mission critical that we evolve alongside the society which continues to evolve outside the office walls.

If we don't adapt, evolve, change - as enterprises operating in the fast-paced, modern world - we die.

Part of this evolution is to get with the programme D&I wise. Today's business and social landscape is a diverse one and, as we now know, the more diversity and inclusive behaviour we have on boards, in teams and within our staff, the wider the perspectives and the better the innovation and ability to seize opportunities and rise to challenges.

I suppose the thing we don't like about change is the uncertainty. We humans are not keen on that. Indeed, uncertainty engages our fight or flight impulse. However, as Jonathan Fields rightly points out in his book on the subject, 'with uncertainty comes possibility'. So, what if we viewed change (and the potential uncertainty that change can bring) in a different way?

What if we focused on the possibilities and opportunities that will arise tomorrow as a direct result of the changes we make today?

What if we focused on the successes that we'll achieve tomorrow as a direct result of the mistakes we make today?

For example, sadly, when one of my businesses went into administration, I was unsure whether I'd recover, not only financially, but emotionally too. However, within a year I was offered a role as an Executive Committee Member for the Institute of Directors, advising on D&I policies. I'm a Company Director of multiple companies and speak regularly on the topic of diversity as well as hosting my own high-profile events to support charitable causes.

So much possibility came from the initial uncertainty. But I learned that, through championing others first and putting myself second, through my podcast and through my new social venture "DIAL GLOBAL", opportunities will abound again if you learn from mistakes and seek possibility amid uncertainty.

This book aims to empower leaders to lead purposefully and optimistically. And it aims to guide leaders through the journey of change into an enriching D&I landscape. A fertile ground where the people thrive, along with the businesses where they feel they truly belong.

I believe a different two-pronged approach is required.

1. **SELF-EMPOWERMENT:** To shift from seeing Diversity and Inclusion as about the under-represented 'victim'

towards minorities and women stepping into their power to speak up; taking ownership by uncovering our strengths and bringing our best selves to the best companies which value us. (And choosing who to work for and with, based on their proactive policies).

2. **LEADERSHIP:** To focus on the issue of leadership, so that current and future leaders can be sufficiently equipped with the tools and the methods that will help each and every person they hire feel seen, heard and valued.

Therefore, this book provides existing and aspiring leaders with a framework for creating a truly inclusive culture within a motivated, engaged and authentic workforce, whilst also providing anyone who has ever felt disconnected or disengaged at work with tools to help them relinquish the pressure of conforming so that they might be free to work more effectively.

It is essentially a wake-up call to transform leaders into beacons of inspiration, transform employees into evangelists and transform organisations into thriving enterprises which a diverse range of people love to work for, where they feel a deep sense of belonging – that integral and hugely motivating yet basic human need.

Chapter 1

Inclusion and Belonging – The Keys to Unlocking a Diverse Workforce

"Every human can think of a moment when he or she felt they didn't belong,"
Anita Sands

Over three decades, D&I has evolved. So much so, it might now perhaps be referred to as D, I & B – Diversity, Inclusion & Belonging. Especially since statistics are showing that simply having a diverse workforce, is not enough.

Mountains of research now exist to suggest that diverse and inclusive teams which foster a sense of belonging make better, quicker decisions and perform better than those which focus on diversity alone.

Today then, diversity without inclusion or belonging is a missed opportunity to engage and retain people who will bring their best selves to work each day. Today, belonging, inclusion and diversity are about removing barriers, restrictions and limitations and widening opportunity, equality and authenticity.

A diverse workplace tells you – you are represented here. You'll find others who like you.

An inclusive space tells you – you are invited to contribute here. You'll be an active participant.

A space strong on belonging tells you – it's okay to be different. We celebrate difference here.
DI&B is no longer just about representation, it's about recognition. It's no longer just about diversity, it's about authenticity. And it's no longer about reactivity, it's about pro-activity. As - Ian John Toal, Chief executive officer, Alfaco previously said: "Inclusion isn't being "liked". It's about being accepted or vaguely appreciated. It's what people want from you too. It's not so difficult to do. It just takes time, effort and consideration."

As podcast interviewee Davide Moro, Marketing VP at Nespresso, says, "Diversity is a fact. Inclusion is a behaviour." One might add to this: belonging is an acceptance; a way of showing up and allowing others to show up.

Indeed, it's been said that 'diversity is what you have' while 'inclusion is what you do'. With that in mind 'belonging' is how we make people feel. Something which, as Maya Angelou, a 'shero' of mine famously says is critical in leadership as it is in life:

"People will forget what you said, people will forget what you did, but people will never forget how you made them feel."

Belonging is a feeling and everyone deserves to *feel* comfortable, at ease and as much at home as the rest of their team. Furthermore, everyone deserves to *feel* encouraged to participate fully and equally as their true whole selves when they come to work, especially given how much time we spend working.

Yes, everyone deserves to belong. Even the fictional David Brent, Ricky Gervais' cringe-worthy character from the office, bless him. His heart's in the right place and, essentially, all he wants is to feel belonging. That's all any of us wants and we need to feel it in order to *feel* engaged as employees (and as leaders) so we may do our best work.

We'll explore more about the importance of the 'whole self' in the next chapter. For now, I want to dive deeper into what inclusion and belonging actually are, what they mean and why they matter so greatly.

The Missing Link

Ever since I first embarked on a career within the D&I arena, I've long felt that the spirit of embracing everyone and winning hearts and minds through inclusive leadership has been of the greatest importance. For me, inclusion has always felt as vital as representation via diversity. Indeed, many leaders today feel the same.

I'm certainly not the only one who has recognised that true D&I (or D,I&B) is about more than merely feeling represented.

"We're still not moving the needle enough," says Former CHRO at LinkedIn, Pat Wadors, who argues that D&I are not sufficient for employee engagement. "Belonging is the missing part of the equation:"

So:

Diversity and Inclusion + Belonging = Engagement

Without inclusion, the innovation and growth that a diverse team holds won't come to fruition. Diversity alone does not drive inclusion. The capability of diversity is unlocked by inclusion and belonging unlocks the capability of inclusion towards engagement. As such, inclusivity and belonging unlock the potential of every member of staff.

"Only when we feel psychologically safe can we unleash our best selves," said Pat in her 2016 Keynote on The Power of Belonging. "When we're part of a team that values our opinion, we speak up and contribute more. Alternatively, when we don't feel like we belong, we lose productivity because we waste time worrying about it. (Minorities spend 25-30% of their time worrying about how they fit in.)"

The benefits of creating a culture of belonging brings to your business are better staff retention, improved performance and increased innovation. Why? Because enhancing people's confidence in their ability to bring their whole self to work is enabling.

Think about it. When you feel comfortable, you feel more able to contribute; to share experiences and express ideas. And the more we enable people to contribute, the more engaged they feel and the more likely they are to stay, to perform to the best of their ability and to come up with the kind of ideas and solutions which will give our organisations the competitive advantage over those who don't create such a culture.

Thankfully, companies are starting to get the message in terms of how they prioritise inclusion and belonging.

As Leendert Den Hollander, VP and GM at Coca-Cola European Partners told me in a recent podcast episode:

"We now call it Inclusion & Diversity and see it more as a philosophy than a strategy". He adds, "We've learnt over the years that we have to put the "i" before the "d."

Teresa Boughey, CEO of Jungle HR, who I also interviewed on my podcast concurs.

"Inclusion is really about creating a sense of belonging. It's where people feel respected and valued within the environment - and they can achieve their true potential. It's the mix, the blend; it's about valuing the unique differences we all have."

In this way:

Diversity is your mix of different people.

Inclusion is how well you enable your people to mix.

Belonging is enabling your people to bring their unique and authentic selves into that mix.

This requires not just having a diverse mix of people and not just the action of inclusion, but the actualisation of acceptance.

For variety is valuable. Each different perspective brings extra value.

When we accept people's differences; the unique traits, perspectives and wisdom which each individual brings to the party, and we allow every single person to dance to their own drumbeat, we provide them with that crucial sense of belonging. And we empower them.

So before we get into the nuts and bolts of belonging, let's define precisely what we mean by these terms.

Diversity is...

Diversity is about uniqueness and recognising our individual differences - This leads to representation. It's about seeing yourself represented and reflected in your organisation's marketing material, on their website, on the board and amongst all the various teams and hierarchies within the business as a whole. It's not only about representing multiple ethnicities and races; it's also about representing different mindsets, genders, age-groups and religions.

Inclusion is...

Inclusion is about connection, participation and encouragement. It's about being welcomed, your viewpoint considered and being invited to participate and contribute, so you may advance and be part of an outcome-shaping team.

Inclusion is the intentional act of cultivating a welcoming environment which enables a variety of different people to thrive. This can only happen when people are invited to contribute and participate, so they have an active and valued role to play as part of something.

I love the Verna Myers quote, which sums up the difference between D&I perfectly:

"Diversity is being invited to the party. Inclusion is being asked to dance."

So, what about belonging?

Belonging is...

For me, belonging is about being able to dance like nobody is watching – to dance *your* way, without inhibition or restriction; enabled to express your true authentic self, no holds barred; to own that dance floor and dance to your own drumbeat!

You can only do that when you feel like you belong. Otherwise, you'd just feel weird.

Belonging is about feeling seen, heard and accepted; knowing that you matter as an essential part of a team, and knowing that you can be your authentic self, without consequence. It's about feeling comfortable enough to remove the mask, shed the armour and just be you, and be accepted as such! It's that feeling that your true authentic and whole self is welcomed, valued and celebrated sufficiently that you can thrive.

So belonging makes you feel safe and comfortable. As such, belonging makes you more likely to want to stay at that party, to keep on dancing and to encourage more people to step onto the dance floor to dance in their own unique way too.

The verb 'belong' applies to being in 'the right place' (i.e. feeling at home) and also to feeling happy or comfortable in a situation (i.e. feeling accepted).

As Abraham Marlow's Hierarchy of Needs reveals, along with our need for food and shelter, human beings have an in-built need to belong. We are wired for belonging; that need to connect and be accepted. These are what I like to call the ABC of D&I – Acceptance, Belonging and Connection.

Maslow's Hierarchy of Needs:

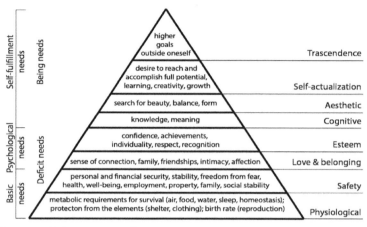

(www.ethicsage.com)

Working environments which foster recognition and reward for individuals as well as teams, provide opportunities to voice ideas and celebrate uniqueness, give people a tangible feeling of belonging.

And those people stay longer at the party.

Indeed, research has shown that working environments which foster a sense of belonging are significantly impacting the bottom line and ensuring that talent is retained.

People are less likely to feel like they belong when they're in the minority, when everyone is different to them, when they are the only person, or one of only a few people, who looks, speak or behave like them; hence the importance of Diversity.

Then, if their voice is excluded from discussions and they're not invited to contribute, they'll feel excluded; hence the importance of Inclusion.

Finally, if there are plenty of people who look or sound like them and they're invited to contribute, yet they still don't feel entirely at home or comfortable or accepted they'll consequently feel like they need to cover up part of themselves, so they may still feel like they don't quite belong. Hence the importance of Belonging as a priority in its own right.

Belonging is a critical part of the whole diversity piece, because it demonstrates that D&I is not just about similarity, it's about uniqueness too. Because it's possible to fit in and stand out at the same time and be alright with that – belonging gives you permission to step into your uniqueness and just be who you are. No mask on, no armouring up, just freedom to be yourself.

And therein lies the key to defining belonging – the freedom to be you rather than who you think you should be.

EXERCISE: Belonging

At some time or another, we've all felt like we didn't fit in; like we didn't belong, whether that was or is at work or at school.

When was the last time you felt like you didn't belong at work? Somewhere else? Jot down your personal story below.

I was at _____

_____

I felt like I didn't belong because_____

_____

It made me feel _____

_____

Now consider a time when you felt different. What happened? How did you feel and what did you do? How did you cope?

_____

_____

_____

_____

_____

This exercise can help you consider how we all feel different and like we don't belong from time to time. We all have that in common. It can work well to do this individually or as part of a group exercise experience as you can relate to each other's experiences.

However, there's an important difference between fitting in and belonging.

Fitting in? Or Belonging?

As master of the mic-drop quote, Brené Brown says:

"The opposite of belonging is fitting in."

She goes on to say:

"Fitting in and belonging are not the same thing and, in fact, fitting in gets in the way of belonging. Fitting in is about assessing a situation and becoming who you need to be to be accepted. Belonging, on the other hand, doesn't require us to change who we are; it requires us to be who we are."

As I said, 'mic-drop!'

As well as flagging up the importance of enabling people to be who they truly are at work, Brené's words demonstrate how part of the D, I & B piece is about developing a culture of acceptance so people don't need to change themselves to fit in. Rather, we need to change our organisations and the way we lead them.

I spent most of my life trying to fit in with lots of different groups at school and nursery, and this continued into my business life. And it's only very recently that I've truly found that it's okay to be different. It's okay to not fit the norm. It's okay not to fit into your classic cookie cutter type mould. It's okay to have a bespoke cookie cutter, and actually to be able to draw strengths from lots of different parts of yourself. Because difference is good!

Similarities and Differences – Tribes and Individuals

This is why D&I is simultaneously about difference and similarity.

On the one hand, we are more likely to feel like we belong and fit in, if there are people like us, similar to us in our places of work. Of course, this doesn't always mean people who have one thing in common with us (race, gender, sexuality) but people who we feel the most kinship and connection with. Perhaps we've got similar stories, having been through similar situations? Perhaps we treat others in the same way and have similar moral characteristics?

Perhaps we share the same sense of humour or personality traits? Either way, in this sense, it's about finding an affinity with people who look, sound, feel or think the same as us – it's about similarity. Because similarity breeds connection and enables us to find our tribe (those who we've identified as sharing our values and goals, for example) which helps us feel like we belong.

Yet, as we know, diversity is also about difference – about focusing on representing a range and variety of different people with different beliefs, values, perspectives and skills across a range of different races, genders and sexual persuasions. So inclusion is about including the individual and celebrating what makes us unique as individuals, not just creating groups, silos or tribes.

As such, it's important to shine a light on both similarities and difference, to cultivate and celebrate both.

As my friend and podcast interviewee Dennis Ossipov-Grodsky, ex-Head of Vayner Consulting and founder of agile5, said to me:

"Each human being is unique. You and I might be born in the same place, our parents might be friends; perhaps they went to the same school. But that collection of instances which created Leila will be infinitely different from the collection of instances that I am constituted of. And that creates a completely unique take on life."

It is these unique takes on life which businesses benefit from. When we tap into a diverse mix of individual perspectives, we broaden our knowledge base, deepen our pot of ideas and create a fountain of innovation and possibility.

"When we listen and celebrate what is both common and different, we become a wiser, more inclusive, and better organisation."
Pat Wadors, ex-Chief of HR at LinkedIn,
Chief Talent Officer at Service Now

EXERCISE: Similarities and Differences

This exercise is for groups to participate in.

Draw a big flower onto a flipchart with a petal to represent each person in the group. Discuss what you each have in common, the similarities that you share and, in the nucleus of the flower, write something(s) that you all have in common.

Next, have each group member write in their own petal what is unique about them, something completely different to every other member of the group, not including physical characteristics.

No matter how similar we are, we can always find unique traits which make us stand out from one another and, no matter how different we are, we can always find similarities that we have in common. Hence the importance of creating diverse teams who can relate to each other, yet have unique perspectives and ways of thinking and showing up in the world.

Individual Think

Oftentimes, when you mention Diversity & Inclusion, in the most basic sense people see this as meaning you should simply hire a diverse mixture of people. This is the first of many steps. It's important for companies to build a jigsaw when they hire; to ensure they don't hire in their own shadows. It's obviously no good to hire exact copies and clones of ourselves – we need to hire people who don't think like us.

During my work in executive search and recruitment, I've seen people hiring others because they like the same football team. I know it sounds ludicrous, but I've seen people who have got the same hobbies and interests, and, because they feel that there is a connection with this individual - despite their skills, they've hired them. Not exclusively because of this, but it's made them more inclined to want to hire that individual, because they're most like them; similar.

That's very dangerous. Because this lack of diversity can often result in group think. And, if you've got group think, you're not going to foster an innovative space where lots of different ways of thinking enter the room together and generate something unique, fresh and magnificent; you're not going to breed a culture where there are lots of different minds around the table – each contributing something different and, therefore, valuable.

Conversely, you'll end up with group think, i.e. the same bunch of output and answers to a problem. That's no good to long term business sustainability, to innovation or to attracting a diverse range of solutions to a business problem.

Far better to hire people different to yourselves, who have skills which complement and who, ideally, have different personalities to yourself. There are different tests and personality indicators available now – from the Belbin test to

Myers Briggs – which help you to gain a much better understanding of people's different personality types and preferences. This enables you to hire a good diverse mixture of people who can each contribute to enable more well-rounded decisions and wider-reaching solutions.

By focusing on our differences, we can find the real treasures that make up each individual, and tap into those unique strengths.

Celebrating Difference

When FT top 10 global future leader and one of the UK's first LGBTQ+ East Asian advocates, Martin Pong, was younger, being different was used as ammunition with which to attack him and put him down.

However, as a result of exploring the importance of D&I, Martin realised he could use his difference to lift him up.

"I understood that my difference was actually one of my most powerful aspects," says Martin.

This is perhaps where so many companies get it wrong with D&I. They want the minorities they employ to feel included, so they feel that they belong and fit in. And they think this can only happen by making sure they hire in lots of people who are similar to them. Ironically, by employing for diversity, they are focusing on only one part of the D,I& B pie – similarity, rather than the part which enables belonging – celebrating difference.

Myself, I was very shy when I was younger. But embracing this work in the field of Diversity, Inclusion and Belonging helped me to come out of my shell and helped me to feel more comfortable in my own skin.

It's a very difficult thing to do - to feel like your true and authentic self, when you're operating within a world that is primarily full of people who are the opposite gender and a different race.

But if I had not recognised that I had a USP myself – that my difference was my power, I would have struggled to succeed in this space.

If I had not been able to embrace my true self and stop trying all the time to fit in, I don't think I would be where I am today. I needed to give myself permission to embrace my vibrant, energetic, enthusiastic personality, without apology, without external approval and use it to my advantage.

Just like we use the Unique Selling Points of products and services to gain competitive advantage in a crowded marketplace, I needed to find my own Unique Selling Point.

Had that not happened, I would not have started to speak out about diversity and inclusion holistically. I wouldn't have been able to have the gravitas to be able to go out there with confidence and speak to these leaders, who are often between 10-30 years older with more experience than I, had I not found and used my difference in a positive way.

By entering the D&I arena, I was able to tell my own personal story about being a Chinese child adopted by British White parents, about embracing my authentic self, about being culturally confused and a little lost. I was able to use my story of not knowing who I was or what my purpose was and how finding D&I essentially allowed me to find my heart; to be myself; to become myself.

If you can become yourself and help those who work alongside you to become themselves too, you'll create a team with originality, sustainability and a power that many teams do not have – the possibility that comes from authenticity.

If you can embrace differences and ensure that every single individual is heard, you'll win the hearts of minds of everyone who works in your organisation.

Celebrating Similarities

Connecting on belief systems and their point of view, accelerates relationships – so uncovering the similarities people share is an important part of the journey towards creating a sense of connection and belonging.

The gold is when people of different nationalities, races, sexual persuasions, genders, backgrounds, cultures and so on work together towards a common goal and shared purpose – that's when the magic really happens. The connection engages people to bring their best selves to the projects they believe in, united as a team and better together.

For example, when Martin Pong realised that the business leaders and colleagues in the companies he was working for had fostered a sense of belonging for him, he felt compelled to do the same for others. "I saw that people around me have taken it upon themselves to make this a safe environment for me. And it felt like a responsibility to continue advocating for that, to ensure it would continue. That's what drives the D&I work I do now," says Martin, "To help the next generation strive together towards a common goal."

Working to a common shared purpose further begets belonging, as we'll explore in a later chapter. This is what unites people who are different to each other and, in a diverse landscape, that's why purpose is so vital.

It also explains why I've never felt more like I belong than I do now – as I write this book and work on creating DIAL Global (Diverse – Inclusive – Aspirational - Leaders), an organisation which puts purpose before profit and serves to harness the power of knowledge and education to inspire, educate and motivate a global community of leaders.

When lots of different people unite with a shared 'why', well that's powerful.

But how do we effectively balance similarities with differences?

Top Tips on Balancing Similarities and Differences in The Workforce

1. **Provide individuals with the chance to spend time together so they may develop mutual respect.** This takes time but it's crucial. When people are dating, they don't decide to marry each other after the first date, they spend time together in order to build that long-term sustainable relationship. The same is true for working relationships. So, give people the chance to get to know the real version of the other person.

2. **Encourage your teams to work with somebody who is different from them** – someone who has a different personality profile, colour, gender, sexuality, different values, opposite preferences – just different in some or many ways. Have them notice differences but also tune in to any synergies.

3. **Seek out the similarities** – not just in characteristics, interests, values or backgrounds but in situations or circumstances (to foster a sense that we're in this together – that powerful unity in shared humanity). For example, the pair may share strong family values, perhaps they have both experienced their parents' divorcing or have been through a similarly painful situation? Or perhaps they share an interest in reading books by a certain author or doing Stand Up Paddleboard Yoga? Maybe they have the same favourite foods? There will be similarities somewhere.

4. **Find and celebrate the differences** – have them each notice and pinpoint their own unique personal strengths. Invite each person to comment to build up different perspectives about each person's individual strengths. What makes them stand out? How might they use their strengths to help others and to help themselves – we'll explore this in more detail in Chapter 4 on Wellbeing.

5. **Focus on building 'bridging' capital (which strengthens ties and solidarity across all groups) as well as 'bonding' capital (which strengthens ties and solidarity within a group).** Political scientist, Robert Putnam suggests that most diversity initiatives focus too much on the latter with business and employee resource groups. Both are important. But, when we seek and find common ground across all groups, we can develop a far healthier community. Conversely when we focus on in-group connection, an 'us and them' mentality can be developed, leading the individuals within the group to remain in silos.

10 Ways To Cultivate a Culture of Belonging

As we've seen, diversity, inclusion and belonging all feed each other. Because, it's not just about feeling valued; it's knowing (and having proof) that you have the same opportunities as everyone else; where colour, culture, sexuality, gender are not restrictive in any way to your advancement. So barriers must be removed.

Pay Attention to the Person Not Just the People

1. **Discuss with staff the barriers they feel may be holding them back from progressing;** those which might make them feel like they don't have the same opportunities as others. For example, there might be a lack of flexibility for working mothers, a lack of sponsors and role models or a restrictive dress code, which makes people fearful of bringing their whole selves to work. Discuss these barriers then make company-wide policy changes which remove these barriers and publicise them among your staff – show you're listening and are committed to cultivating a culture of belonging and equal opportunities for all. As VP Marketing at Nespresso, Davide Moro, says: *"The basic foundational inclusive behaviour you need to have is to care. The common ground is to allow everyone to have the same chances, and be treated in the same way."*

2. **Invite storytelling and show a genuine interest in the stories and personal circumstances of each person who works for you** – from interview phase onwards. That means giving them a voice and listening to it. When people share their stories, they give you a chance to be drawn into their world, to see things from their perspective, to see the real them. And you give

them a chance to hide from personal circumstances less and engage more. The sharing and hearing of stories bolsters understanding of people's strengths and journeys and builds empathy for them as individuals – the result is a deeper sense of belonging.

3. **Allow conversations to be held on sensitive topics -** by hosting events where people can talk about circumstances and issues which are affecting them.

4. **Ensure individuals share the credit in the success of their team.** Offer constant recognition for each person's contribution and celebrate every success to enable pride in their position within the team. Show them you see they are doing a great job and acknowledge this. When you recognise people for their accomplishments, give them the chance to freely express their opinions and ideas and demonstrate their contributions in team meetings are valued, they feel like they belong.

5. **Invest in their connection. Unite and connect geographically-dispersed teams**. Yes, tap into the technology which brings people together, such as Zoom or other virtual meeting software. But consider investing in annual face-to-face retreats where your people can connect and collaborate in person. The return on such an investment comes in the form of stronger and more aligned working relationships with deeper meaningful connection, heightened employee

engagement and long-term productivity, good staff retention and harmony in the workplace.

6. **Ensure there are sufficient role models for people to look up to so they have a definition of what is attainable to them career-wise.** Give people an idea of what success looks like and show them it looks like them. During a recent podcast I had the opportunity to interview News Presenter and Correspondent, Clive Myrie who said *"You need a living example that your dream can come true. The crucial role model for me was Sir Trevor McDonald who lead by example. I thought, if he can do it maybe I can too?"* However, as Clive reflects, more needs to be done here. Says Clive, *"The sad thing is, there is still only a handful of black frontline presenters and correspondents."* When we don't see people who look and sound like us, we feel less able or like it's less likely that we'll succeed. Role models give people a 'well if she can do it, so could I' mindset of possibility. I remember Martin Pong telling me that, growing up, the only high-profile person who had any kind of resemblance to him was Gok Wan and I thought, "Yes! Me too!" We discussed how this lack of individuals who look like us on TV might have to do with a cultural reason, such as being encouraged to strive to be doctors or lawyers, rather than TV presenters.

7. **Vocalise your values and don't stay silent about topics which you care about** – share the company's

position and opinion on what's right and wrong. Remember, silence speaks volumes. Stand up for causes you believe in and against issues which you feel need addressing, those which tie in to your own values. This provides a moral compass and level of trust which people can use to figure out whether they are likely to be supported in this company. As Jennifer Brown, speaker, author and D&I expert told me, "Our employees are looking to leadership to say, 'Do you see me? Do you care about me and what's impacting me outside of the workplace?'"

8. **Be a listening leader. (Provide opportunities for individuals to speak and ensure they are heard.** Make people feel comfortable and safe when proposing new ideas and expressing their views. Enable people to make decisions. Have regular conversations. Give, request and implement feedback.) (We'll explore the need for leaders to listen in Chapter 3). – As Ian John Toal, Chief executive officer, Alfaco says "I believe that no matter where you're from that you can all make a huge difference, but only if you respect and listen to everyone."

9. **Cultivate an open-minded workforce by focusing on curiosity over judgement.** Acceptance of others enables us also to build our own sense of self-acceptance and belonging. When leaders create a culture where alternative views, all views, are considered, it paves the way for us, as individuals, to

recognise and accept that different views exist, and to open our minds to the notion of every individual's opinion being of value. If we get curious and choose curiosity and our ability to notice our own thought patterns and internal prejudices, we can open ourselves up to wider possibilities and to greater acceptance.

10. **Set up a photo sharing group and provide the group with daily prompts.** This is a wonderful way to spark curiosity and conversation and provides a platform for people to share a little more of themselves. For example, prompts might include: '#work,' '#rest', '#play', '#community', '#love', '#colour', '#pattern', '#shape', '#pause' '#hidden', '#revealed', '#self' and so on. Invite people to share their photos along with a short explanation about that photo and what the prompt word means to them.

"Good leadership requires you to surround yourself with people of diverse perspectives who can disagree with you without fear of retaliation,"
Doris Kearns Goodwin

"In strong companies best ideas win; not egos, not politics,"
Oleg Vishnepolsky

What Happens When People Feel They DO Belong?

According to research by the Centre for Talent Innovation, "Employees who are able to bring their whole selves to work are 42% less likely to say they intend to leave their job within a year. Those with sponsors are 62% more likely to have asked for and have received a promotion. And 69% of women who off-ramp would have stayed at their companies if they'd had flexible work options."

So, when people feel like they belong, they'll stay with an organisation, they'll perform far better within their teams and individually.

As a report on Inclusive Leadership across six countries, suggests: "Employees who feel included report higher levels of innovation and team citizenship." The same is true in schools, as an Organisation for Economic Cooperation and Development report found that people with a greater sense of belonging had a higher level of engagement and academic performance.

Indeed, piles of research over the past two decades, demonstrates that both pupils and employees perform better and retain more information when they feel part of something. This also feeds into why purpose matters, which we'll cover later in the book.

Furthermore, when people feel at home in an organisation themselves, they tend to show more acceptance and compassion to others within the organisation. Belonging therefore, not only has a positive impact on performance, but on the wider culture of the business.

Showing people they belong motivates them.

The danger for businesses today, is when we don't.

What Happens When People Feel They DON'T Belong?

There's a science of belonging which has proven that:

Our brains don't work as well when we feel excluded.
Our brains work better when we feel included!

Drop-out rates and poor academic performance in colleges, as reported by *The Journal of Experimental Education* correlated with a lack of belonging.

The same is true in the workplace.

Outsiders or people who feel excluded from a group devote their mental energy to scan the environment and monitor for threats, such as discrimination, barriers and assumptions around stereotypes. That's what we're wired to do. The 'unusual suspects' among us consequently have less energy left to devote to higher cognitive processes, such as decision-making and innovating. However, this is only when we feel like we don't belong.

This has been proven in experiments with Black students when they performed better in standardized tests scores when race wasn't mentioned, compared to when it was.

According to social psychologist, Claude Steele, "'Stereotype threat' is when people feel at risk of confirming, as self-characteristic, a negative stereotype" about their race, gender, ethnicity and so on.

And, as our fight or flight response kicks in, when our stereotypes are highlighted and we feel a lack of belonging to the majority group as a result, our performance tends to weaken.

So it's no good hiring in your token Black people or Asian people and establishing women's groups and LGBTQ+ groups and, in doing so, creating silos. Nor is it helpful to refer in any way to stereotypes of such groups. Doing so will harm the performance of those groups.

It's detrimental to people's performance when they feel aware of being viewed (and likely judged) through the lens of a stereotype. This has been shown to reduce working memory capacity and increase stress and anxiety.

A black person doesn't want to confirm a stereotype any more than a blonde woman does. Stereotypes are limiting. They offer a restricted view of the world and of individuals. Not only that, they impede our performance and, as we'll explore in the following chapter, they make us waste our energy on the wrong kind of performing, i.e. performing by pretending to be less like ourselves rather than performing by doing our best work as ourselves.

EXERCISE: Identity

Think about what you consider to be the most important areas of your own identity.

Write your name in the centre of a piece of paper and then draw circles around it. In each circle write down descriptive words which relate to your identity. For example, Female, Painter, Asian, Sister, Entrepreneur, Working Class, Reader, Swimmer.

Which areas and words are you proud of? Write down or share a story about a time when you've been proud to be part of a particular group.

_____

_____

_____

Now write down or share a story about a time when you were embarrassed or found it hurtful to be associated with a particular group and write down some stereotypes about this group.

_____

_____

_____

Write down or share a story about a time when you have found you've 'covered' up an authentic part of your identity in order to conform or fit in.

_____

_____

_____

Next, in groups, invite participants to draw a line down the middle of a piece of paper.

At the top of the first column, ask them to write, "I Am."
At the top of the second column, ask them to write, "I Am Not."
In between the two columns have them write the word, 'But'.

So it should read: "I Am _____ But, I Am Not _____.
Ask each group member to fill in the blanks with something which identifies them based on their race, religion or sexuality and fill in the second blank with a common stereotype about that group which isn't true of them. For example, I am blonde, but I am not unintelligent or I am Asian, but I am not a maths whizz.

Share the statements and discuss stereotypes and how they are limiting and restrictive to individuality.

Potential Limitations

According to social neuroscience reports, the social threat of disconnection and stereotype affiliation is processed by the brain in the same way as the threat of physical harm. The stress hormone, cortisol, is released and our cognitive abilities are adversely affected.

As business leaders we want our people to fulfil their full potential, do their best for the company and thrive. Yet, when they don't feel a sense of belonging, that's not possible.

Evidently, it's in everyone's interest to foster an inclusive culture where every single individual feels like they belong.

It's difficult enough for people with 'dual' cultures to feel that. So anything we, as business leaders, can do to cultivate belonging is key.

Take my friend and podcast interviewee, Martin Pong.

Both of his parents arrived in Manchester from Hong Kong to study at University. He spoke Cantonese at home and English at school: "Very early on I noticed this divide. It was like I was dividing my identity and I began to understand what it meant growing up as an actual minority in the UK."

Overtime, after having the mickey taken out of him for being different one part of that identity began to suffer. Martin recalls, "I started associating a lot of negativity with my Chinese identity. And over time, that impacted me a lot. I worked hard to detach myself from that part of who I am".

It was only when he started at University and met a more diverse set of people that he was able to reconnect with his heritage and family traditions once more – and start to piece together his identity. But it is only through working as an LGBTQ+ and ethnic minority intersectional advocate that

Martin has finally begun to feel able to show up as his whole self – to become whole again. Unfortunately for many, this negative association with the part of an identity which brings with it troubling situations (through bullying, discrimination or a lack of belonging) can continue on through your life. As a result, you don't bring your whole self to work.
And what a waste that is!

I can relate to Martin's story. Although I was adopted by British parents in Hong Kong and therefore have White British parents rather than Immigrant parents, my brother Michael and I are Chinese. We've never spoken the language, but I still looked very different. The times I wished that I had blonde hair and blue eyes and longed to fit in and be the same as them, rather than different, were many.

That was a big turning point for me at University," says Martin, "when I finally understood what it felt like to be in that safe and inclusive environment, where I felt like I belonged. This coincided with the time when I understood what it meant to be LGBTQ+. I wouldn't have been able to do that if it, if the environment wasn't as inclusive as it was."

For Martin, feeling that sense of inclusion and belonging enabled him not only to reconnect with his Chinese self, but also enabled him to explore the LGBTQ+ part of his identity – to really uncover his true whole authentic self.

And that, Dear Reader, is what drives belonging – feeling safe, welcome and comfortable as OURSELVES.

Chapter 2
The Whole Self and The Importance of Authenticity

"Why fit in when you were born to stand out?"
Dr. Seuss

Labels may group us together with others 'like us', yet they separate rather than unify. They separate us from those 'unlike us' but also assume that, because we share one attribute we are, somehow, the same.

Yet there is a multiplicity within each of our identities – our whole selves and it is this – your whole self, my whole self – which should be valued and accepted and enabled and empowered wherever we choose to put ourselves to work.

Because it is this, our whole selves, which determines how we show up in the world; how we operate and how we integrate and interact with the world around us.

It is our whole selves: our strengths, weaknesses, likes, dislikes, experiences, ideas, culture, values, successes, failures, almighty mistakes (of which we've all made many) and lessons learned, which shape who each of us is entirely and inform how we work and, indeed, how we lead – as individuals.

When a place of work, a place where we devote the majority of our time and effort, requires us (knowingly or unknowingly) to choose between the multiplicity of our individual identities in order to conform, this prevents each of us from behaving authentically, so we can't truly bring who we are – our whole selves – to the table, and nobody benefits from that.

> *"It takes a lot of energy to be someone you are not"*
> **Unknown**

Semi-self is a lose-lose situation. Because you don't get the best of your people when they spend their working lives being half of themselves and devoting the rest of their energy to covering up the part of them which doesn't conform to those outdated dictums. Unfortunately, this is the status quo for many people working in organisations today.

Yet you and I are so much more and we have so much more to give. Embrace that and we all win.

Indeed, being able to participate and perform well in the workplace has a lot more to do with our ability to show up as our authentic selves than we realise. It affects our energy and how much we have to devote to our job; it affects our ability to do our job to the best of our ability, it affects how much we feel a sense of belonging and it affects our working relationships.

Authentic Connections

Authenticity is crucial, not only when it comes to belonging, but also when it comes to connection. It's harder to get to know you if you're not really being you at all.

Frankly, I find it difficult to build a strong long-lasting connection with someone if they're not being authentic. As such, it's so important for people to be who they truly are; accepted as their true authentic selves.

Of course, there's a perpetual loop in action here – only when we're accepted as our true authentic selves can we feel comfortable showing up as our true authentic selves. So we can only wholly show up when we feel like we belong.

And, if authenticity is so crucial to connecting with others and building strong relationships with them, this means belonging is crucial to enabling that authenticity, and thus, that connection - between people. That goes for building strong relationships between your staff members, their teams, their customers and clients and all stakeholders in your business.

The authenticity of personally connecting with individuals can really help accelerate relationships. And good relationships can mean the difference between business success and failure.

Championing a Culture of Authenticity

As a leader you want your people to devote their energies to performing to the best of their abilities, not to performing an act they feel they need to keep up in order to fit in.

Putting on a performance doesn't equate to giving an optimum performance.

They can only give their best performance when they are free to be themselves!

When we hire people, we don't ask them to leave part of themselves at home. We want them to show up as themselves, their best selves, their whole selves. And yet, the pressures society puts on everyone to conform, along with the internal corporate pressure to fit in, can lead the people we've gone to the trouble of interviewing and shortlisting and hiring and training to only partially show up. This chapter explores what we can do about this.

Conversely, when leaders do all that they can to enable authenticity in action, everybody wins. And that's why leaders renowned for their good work in the D&I arena continue to inspire.

Take Dennis Ossipov-Grodsky and Gary Vaynerchuk for example. Dennis is a global business executive with 20 years of entrepreneurial, Fortune top 30 and digital agency experience spanning five continents who went from managing his own small firm in the Ukraine with 10 people to managing 100 at VaynerMedia.

During our podcast conversation, Dennis revealed he constantly asks himself, "How can I become a better manager for my teams? How can I motivate people? What makes them tick?" Over 20 years he's come to realise the main reason people show up as themselves at work is because of other people (and how they make them feel – back to Maya Angelou). He noticed this at Proctor & Gamble, "because we had a very unique culture of growing from within." And again, at Vayner Media, with Gary Vaynerchuk.

"Gary was able to create this environment where people could be themselves – where they were able to show their human side, where they became friends with each other. And that is what brings people into the office and opens up their best self – enabling that authenticity to connect as themselves."

Of course, the alternative is to carry on paying lip service with basic D&I initiatives which lack a focus on authenticity. But, in that instance, you'll find what will happen is that people won't show up fully and, consequently, your business will suffer.

What's more, it can be exhausting for us to operate optimally when we are not being our true selves and when we're putting all of our energy into trying to be who others want us to be. Essentially, when this happens, we are diverting our valuable source of energy away from the work, when it could be utilized into bolstering our productivity, so we may focus intently on delivering the task at hand, rather on trying to be someone we're not.

Shaping who you are to suit someone else – in any relationship – is tiring and difficult to sustain over the long-term. It's far more liberating and empowering to show up with integrity, as yourself.

The truth is, when you feel like you belong, you have nothing to hide, nothing to cover up. When you don't, covering becomes the norm, and it's a very tiring and restrictive place to be.

Conformity and Covering

We all feel the pressure to conform to various extents. Society has trained us to do so. As a result, people cover parts of themselves in order to fit in to existing norms. But some people feel the need to do so more than others.

According to research by the Centre for Talent Innovation, 37% of African-Americans and Hispanics and 45% of Asians say they "need to compromise their authenticity" to conform to their company's standards of demeanour or style.

Meanwhile there has been sufficient research on women in STEM to suggest that acting "like a man" can be advantageous in becoming a leader in these fields.

This pressure to conform and the consequential "covering" is causing D&I efforts to stall.

At Deloitte University a study into a new 'Uncovering Talent' model of inclusion in 2015 looked into addressing this pressure to conform for "historically underrepresented groups", but also for "the straight white men who have traditionally been left out of the inclusion paradigm" who would equally benefit from a culture of authenticity.

The study explored the notion of 'covering' – a term coined by sociologist Erving Goffman in 1963 to define how people, but especially those with "stigmatized identities" made a "great effort to keep the stigma from looming large."

Whereas the term 'passing' means hiding a part of an identity, such as sexuality or disability, 'covering' is different. Covering is about toning down the significance of that identity. Covering is something that all groups have the capacity to do, whereas passing is not.

By way of example, Goffman relayed how, before his Cabinet entered the room, President Franklin Delano Roosevelt would always make sure he was seated behind a table. Everyone was aware that he was in a wheelchair, so he wasn't hiding his disability. He was covering, to ensure his disability was not at the forefront of the interaction. Rather, this part of his identity remained in the background. This is a great historic example of early covering.

Four decades later, University Law Professor, Kenji Yoshino developed the 'covering' concept further by defining ways in which people tend to 'cover' in order to 'fit in' and conform.

1. **Appearance** – Altering what they look like via their attire, grooming and mannerisms, so they may 'fit in' to the mainstream majority. For instance, a gay man might dress in dowdy colours to downplay his sexuality or a black woman might straighten her hair, rather than wear it naturally, to mute the significance ofher race.

2. **Affiliation** – Avoiding stereotypical behaviours which are associated with their identity, such as eating less spicy food or talking less about parenting.

3. **Advocacy** – Choosing not to defend a group of people rather than stick up for them. For example, a Muslim woman might opt not to voice her knowledge or awareness about cultural dress in a conversation about the hijab.

4. **Association** – Avoiding contact with other group members. So a gay woman might choose to leave her wife at home rather than have her attend a work function. Or a disabled man might avoid talking to another person with disabilities over lunch.

All of these covering 'axes' are linked to the fear of being excluded and marginalised; fear of standing out for being different and the consequential fear of being affiliated with a minority group.

And, according to Deloitte University's report, 61% of 3129 respondents across multiple ages, genders, races and orientations reported covering at work, all of them working for organisations with D&I initiatives in place. Take that in for a moment – the majority of all respondents, regardless of race, gender and orientation admitted to 'covering' at work, even though ALL of the companies they worked for were committed to D&I. Evidently there is much work to be done.

Those most likely to cover were LGBTQ+ individuals, 83 per cent of whom reported covering, compared to 79 per cent of Blacks, 66 percent of women, 63 percent of Hispanics and 45 percent of straight White men.

While this survey demonstrates that we all cover to certain extents in order to fit in, it's crucial to note that different groups are singled out for different reasons. For example, Black women were the only subgroup to declare embarrassment about wearing their hair natural and White people didn't avoid public association with other White people, only Black people expressed this avoidance.

None of the respondents felt excluded from work situations. Indeed, they felt included.

However, they still felt compelled to cover parts of their identity so that the more dominant groups wouldn't need to process those aspects. As such, they felt they needed to manage their identities, alongside managing their roles – expending energy on doing so, which is draining.

It's a bit like repressing our emotions – it's damaging as it comes out in other ways, such as through stress and anxiety.

Furthermore, when our energy is expended on masking parts of our personality, that energy is not directed to doing our jobs. In this way masking our true and whole selves is costly for the businesses we work for.

Yet covering is rife across all industries and includes everything from women avoiding talking about motherhood and parental commitments to black women straightening their hair to detract the focus away from those definitive features; from leaving a walking stick at home, to gay men wearing more masculine clothes and downplaying an interest in feminine or flamboyant things; or from gay women leaving personal pronouns out of a discussion to leaving photographs of a same-sex husband or wife at home; from choosing not to correct jokes about Asian or Black stereotypes to avoiding sponsoring the same gender or race as you, for fear of a perception of favouritism.

In this way, covering not only wastes the energy we should be using on doing our jobs on managing our identity instead. Covering is also detrimental to an individuals' sense of self and can result in them feeling less committed to their role and the company they work for, especially when they know they don't fit the mould of leadership and therefore feel restricted in terms of their advancement opportunities.

And, fundamentally, to inhabit a place where you choose silence over voicing an opinion because you don't want to be associated with a stereotype– that limits your potential to shine. When you feel like you can't fully show up, you're essentially losing your voice.

Thankfully, work is being done to further understand the consequences of covering and how we can help our people recover their voices by uncovering their true selves.

For example, after carrying out significant research, the Deloitte University survey sought to understand how organisations can help their employees to 'uncover' and suggests that a company "should consider its values as a touchstone."

Imagine if all leaders created 'authenticity in action' programmes to enable our people to bring their whole selves to work?

This is possible and it starts with implementing this two-step initiative which enables discovery and assessment leading to a reduction in the need to 'cover'.

1. **Discover**: In order to uncover the talent in your organisation, and enable people to uncover rather than cover, you first need to uncover the extent of covering and discover what types of covering take place within your own organisation. You might use surveys to pose questions about how different groups

cover their true authentic selves and why they feel the need to do so?

Only once you've considered these instances and reflected on the impact they have on your organisation, can you seek to do something about it; to create a culture where your people feel able to be their uncovered selves and bring their whole selves into work each day.

2. **Assess**: Once you know who is covering, when they are covering and why so, you can then assess whether your practices and your culture live up to your values and analyse whether there's any conflict between them. Let's say you have strong corporate values of inclusion and gender equality yet many female managers feel obliged to cover in order to progress professionally, you'll need to address this issue.

It's important to uncover the concept of covering with your staff, to get it out into the open, because it enables empathy and a better understanding of each other, i.e. it fosters authenticity in action. Indeed, the work on covering carried out by Deloitte sought to help people better understand how each group covers to foster deeper empathy across groups – a 'we're in this together' kind of unity which comes from knowing 'we all cover' rather than 'they cover.' It also sought to help encourage all groups to want to develop a more authentic culture.

Remember the Brené Brown quote about how belonging "doesn't require us to change who we are; it requires us to be who we are?"

That is essentially what uncovering enables people to take ownership of – to be fully who they are.

So, while inclusion and belonging offer an invitation to "come in", covering offers an invitation to "come out" and this isn't about coming out to announce a sexual orientation, but coming out into the open as YOURSELF.

Of course, the best way to address covering and a conflict between values and practice is for leaders to lead the way by uncovering themselves first, which we'll explore in detail in the next chapter.

For, if we're going to enable the people who work for and with us to be their authentic selves, we need to show up as our authentic selves too.

And that, Dear Reader, takes guts. It takes the courage to step into your vulnerability and share who you truly are – but then, it takes guts to be the emotionally intelligent Leader required to run a successful organisation today.

Chapter 3
How to Lead Well

"In the past, jobs were about muscles, now they're about brains, but in the future they'll be about the heart."

Minouche Shafik, Director, London School of Economics

In a volatile, uncertain and increasingly complex business landscape, where only a quarter of workers feel engaged*, to get the most from their best asset – their people – today's leaders must:

- Build TRUST
- Cultivate CONNECTION
- Develop EMPATHY

Easy to say, but less easy to do, especially when there's so much involved in a leader's day-to-day role in leading themselves, their people and their organisations. Perhaps the most important role though, is role model. And to excel at *that*, leaders need to lead by example.

Lead by Example

As leaders, we all want to get the best from their people, but, frankly, our people are not at their best if they're unable to be who they are; if they're devoting energy to covering up their true selves rather than devoting that energy to their job. As we've learned, covering is draining, uncovering is liberating.

So how do leaders get people to be authentic and to open up?

By opening up themselves first.

Of course, when we think of Executive Leadership, we don't think of vulnerability; that's not the image leadership conveys. We think instead of power and strength, but not vulnerability, which is why it can feel so uncomfortable to lead the way in being so.

Yet therein lies the key – good leadership is about leading the way; it's about going first, it's about saying, 'look everyone, I'm opening up, I'm getting vulnerable, and it's safe. Now you go.' *That's* courageous and authentic leadership!

When leaders lead by example in this way, it has an incredibly positive domino effect as three things happen:

1. We get to know ourselves even better and show up more authentically from that moment onwards....
2. ...Which builds trust...
3. ... Which opens up the conversation to empower others to uncover too.

Once we've opened up about who *we* are, we're so much better positioned to find out more about who everyone else is.

Once we've shared our own humanity, we enable others to do the same. We can open dialogue which leads to a far better understanding of who each individual is, rather than merely what they can do.

Once we've shared our own stories, we open the doors for others to share theirs, which is how we get the best out of our people. That's the secret sauce.

And this lays the foundation for building belonging, developing trust and deepening connection.

The truth is, people who show up authentically inspire more and connect better.

Consequently, when leaders share their own stories of 'uncovering', it eases the process of uncovering for everyone else. It removes the pressure and enables staff to relate on a deeper human level to the people they work for and with.

Indeed, leading by example by uncovering first is probably the most effective way to create a culture of acceptance and belonging, because it fosters a 'we're in this together' mentality and an open-communicative culture. This united vibe can instantly put people at ease and make them feel more comfortable about sharing what would usually feel uncomfortable.

Sharing your vulnerability and your imperfectly flawed self is so important – both as a business leader and as a member of staff, but mostly, as a human being, which all of us have in common. If you stripped everything away, we would simply be hearts and souls.

Uncovering first may feel like stepping in to the unknown, but uncertainty is a part of the leadership landscape. It takes a great deal of bravery to stand up and face into the unknown, but our organisations, our teams and ourselves grow as a result.

> *"What happens when people open their hearts?"*
> *"They get better."*
> **Haruki Murakami**

Case Study: Jennifer Brown's Vulnerability Ripple Effect

Jennifer Brown, author of *Inclusion* and regular keynote speaker, uncovers herself as a member of the LGBTQ+ community on a regular basis in front of every new audience she speaks to. It's vulnerable and yet incredibly effective and empowering. Her legacy is impressive as she's guided so many people towards relinquishing the shackles of covering, to step into their true selves.

As Jennifer relayed to me in my podcast:

"When I stand on stage and come out every single time, it's sometimes uncomfortable for me, particularly when it's in front of 1,000 people or in front of a mostly male audience, as it often is.

I feel vulnerable in those moments, but I remind myself that it's critical for me to show my full self, because it may shine a light on somebody else's experience who's not able to use their voice like I can. So, that momentary discomfort for me could provide a literally life-saving beacon for someone else who's struggling with who they are and struggling with feelings of acceptance, to help them thrive as well."

That's service. That's the kind of leadership we should be championing today: the kind of leadership which involves opening up and, in doing so, serving others.

Jennifer has a wonderful way of demonstrating that we should never judge a book by its cover. As a speaker she "keeps the surprises coming" and "keeps the cognitive dissonance going" by sharing her own stories which "create wonderful moments where people's own biases are challenged."

This elicits such interesting reactions from her audiences, which gets them thinking and sparks conversations about unconscious bias, vulnerability and uncovering.

As Jennifer, who trained as an opera singer before her voice was injured explains:

"I walk on stage and play myself singing with an orchestra - and nobody thinks it's me. So the first thing I say is, "The voice you've just heard was mine." And I take a curtsy, and people think, 'That's not what I thought an opera singer looks like. She's so small, how did she make that noise?' So that's the first surprise."

"Coming out is the second surprise," laughs Jennifer.

"And the surprises keep coming. I say to the audience, 'I walked on stage and you might have thought to yourself, 'Really? This is our diversity speaker?' So I ask them what they think a diverse person looks like? What does an expert look like in the space? They might have thought, 'Here's a white woman, so what does she have to say about this topic?'

Then, when I come out, sometimes, it gets very quiet in the room. But I can feel everyone is hanging on every moment, which gives the conversation power to open up. When people's minds are open and they realise they'd made all kinds of assumptions based on their unconscious biases, which causes a different reaction of, 'Whoa, she knows something I don't know.' So they go with you on this journey and that's fun."

Imagine if every leader reading this book does the same as Jennifer has done – if we could all step up to the parapet, no matter how uncomfortable it may feel, to share our own story – to uncover ourselves, imagine the shift in acceptance and belonging in our organisations and the wider potential ripple effect of that shift?

Safety in Numbers

Part of the compounding impact of this strategy is letting people know: 'you're not alone', 'we're in this together.'

When Jennifer initially went into her boss's office and said, 'right, this is who I am,' she was surprised to realise how uncovering made her feel safer than when she was guarded.

Removing her armour removed her fear.

When you open up, others become more open to you, respectful of you and trusting in you.

As Jennifer points out:
"Remember, you're never alone; your experience is not unique to you. We now have a lot of data and research around how women feel in the workplace, how women of colour, in a different way, feel in the workplace, how a variety of diverse people feel. So now we can say, yes, I feel that way too."

The value of storytelling here is twofold.

First, it's cathartic and, as Jennifer says, "It gets easier over time; that's part of the healing." Consequently, our stories become our tools. "You become - in a way - the master of the story, because it's something you're using intentionally."

Secondly, that intention holds value – to inspire others to show up fully, just as you are now doing. With each story shared, there's this domino effect of barriers being knocked down, thus empowering and enabling each person to step fully into their truest and best selves and show up authentically.

Jennifer's speeches illustrate this positive domino effect:

"Sharing so vulnerably gives other people permission to do the same. So, by the time I unleash delegates into their table groups to share their own examples [of covering] every single time, the room just erupts."

This simply demonstrates how keen people are to be given permission to verbalise something they've not verbalised before to a total stranger who, despite having never met them, totally gets where they're coming from.

The resulting trust Jennifer notices between people is palpable: "It's this really deep transformative movement."

Imagine if we could all enable that transformation within our own places of work, by setting the tone for a safe environment? All we need to do is lead by example, uncover first and give everyone else permission to follow suit?

As Brené Brown so rightly says, "Owning our story can be hard but not nearly as difficult as spending our lives running from it."

Doing so greatly inspires our teams and opens the doors to connection. After all, we all want to see the whole leader. As Jennifer says, "Millennials, in particular, crave that humanity of imperfection and authenticity."

Says Jennifer: "Authenticity means confessing that you don't always have the answer to everything, that you aren't this unassailable leader with no struggles or challenges. But many executive leaders don't. They have these stories, but they never talk about them."

However, as any leader who has stepped up to share their imperfections and vulnerability knows, ownership of these stories unites and inspires. And the stories Jennifer gets to hear demonstrates that even white male leaders have something in common with those who cover the most. They just cover different things in different ways, but we all cover. So sharing these stories leads the way towards a whole company of people who show up to work as their whole best selves. And that's golden.

Ultimately then, whether our diversities are visible or invisible, each day we make a choice about whether to cover those aspects of who we are or uncover them. But we are so much more likely to reveal them when we trust the people we work with, when we trust the environment in which we work.

So, what are you waiting for? Write down your story and go out there and share it, film it, get it in front of your people and watch the domino effect of authenticity in action.

Tell people:

How has exclusion felt in your life?
How has feeling different felt in your life?
How has feeling like an imposter felt in your life?
How has feeling like you have to conform felt in your life?
How is all of this negatively impacting your significance, your contribution, your potential?

In doing so, not only will you grow, but so will your business.

As statistics reveal, those who are enabled to be authentic at work are more engaged and productive. We just need to give people the opportunity to share their personal stories so we can gain a better picture and understanding of how they feel when they come to work.

EXERCISE: Only Human

In a group, invite everyone to take it in turns finishing this sentence with something which shows they are 'only human'.... "If you really knew me, you'd know that..." For example, "... I get anxious when I'm driving to somewhere I've not been before and need everyone in the car to be quiet if the sat nav re-routes." Or "... I've spent so much of my life being late for everything I now set my clocks and watch 15 minutes early."

Repeat the exercise with them finishing the sentence with something that's been on their mind recently. For example, "... my mother isn't well at the moment, so I'm struggling to focus at work."

Next, repeat the exercise with participants finishing the sentence with something that they sometimes feel they need to cover or hide, in order to fit in. For example, "... I straighten my hair for work," or, "...I'm not always as confident as I appear and often worry what people think of me."

Next, repeat the exercise with everyone finishing the sentence to reveal a hidden talent or party trick they may have. For example, "I can juggle and once did a circus skills course," or, "I can do the splits both ways." (A demonstration is often a fun inclusion).

Finally, repeat the exercise with participants finishing the sentence with a fun revelation. For example, "... my guilty TV pleasure is watching America's Next Top Model," or "... When driving in the dark I often switch the car radio to Absolute 80s and sing at the top of my voice."

This is a great exercise for revealing parts of us which we often may cover or hide and demonstrating that we all have vulnerabilities and parts of our selves which people may not know about. It also shows that we all have unique talents; that we are often concerned about similar things, which provides an opportunity to lead into a conversation about covering and authenticity; about showing up as our true selves.

Case Study: Coca-Cola

Coca-Cola has such a diverse portfolio selling to big supermarkets, small corner shops, airlines, leisure parks, all of which sell their drinks to a diverse range of consumers. Having focused on diversity, discussing issues, opportunities and challenges, running a women's network and so on, Vice President & General Manager at Coca-Cola European Partners, Leendert Den Hollander, discovered that, despite the great intent, action and passion, "it didn't really move the needle."

Says Leendert, "That was when we realised, it's not just about diversity; it's about an inclusive culture. And, despite the scientific studies that tell you that inclusive businesses have better results, that doesn't tell you how it feels in a daily operation. How does it *feel* as an employee to work in our company? So we tried to identify what it really feels like."

The company surveyed individuals across different levels of seniority, across different departments and global locations to pin down the values behind Inclusion & Diversity which became a strapline: *"Be Yourself, Be Valued, and Belong."*

The next step was to make that practical and measurable. 100 different people were brought together to answer the question: When was the last time you felt excluded?

"That was a powerful exercise," says Leendert. "Whether it was in a meeting or an event, people felt excluded. So leaders kept asking the questions: "Did your team today feel a bit more inclusive versus yesterday, and what has been your role as a leader to foster that?"

When asked to share when he felt excluded himself, Leendert told me that moving to a new role for a new company in a new country, where he was the only foreigner, gave him that uncomfortable feeling. But he found that useful. Experiencing that feeling enabled him to reflect on what it might be like to feel that way by default on a more regular basis.

Consequently, the company takes action to regularly talk through ways they can minimise or remove those feelings of exclusion; to give each individual the chance to speak up in meetings and openly share whenever they are feeling excluded.

Says Leendert, "People would look at me and ask, 'who is this funny man from Holland with his funny accent?' I recognised that and realised they might not know what was important to me, what I had come to do and not do, where I was coming from. So I tried to connect with people. I found, if you open up, other people will open up too."

Opening Up Opens The Door To Connection

Martin Pong concurs with the knock-on effect of being more open. In fact, Martin cites this openness in sharing his story as the secret of his success in business.

He told me in our podcast conversation:
"Emotionally connecting with people is so important. We've all been in the situation where someone is trying to lead a room, and there's nothing behind the words they're speaking, which makes it difficult to connect or follow them. Whereas, emotionally connecting with people has the opposite effect. And the way to emotionally connect is by showing humility and vulnerability by sharing parts of your story, your emotions and feelings. There shouldn't be a problem sharing those with people, because we all feel them. And it's a powerful way for people to connect on a basic human level."

Indeed, as Kristen Neff's work on compassion reveals, a core component of compassion for others and for ourselves is to remind ourselves of our shared common humanity – we all make mistakes, we all have insecurities and we all feel emotions. As such, admitting when something upsets you, or when you find something challenging is not weak, it's courageous. And it invigorates a sense of humanity, compassion and soul into leadership.

The problem is, our default human setting is to focus on presenting our showreels, our best bits, which everyone then compares to their blooper reels, their best bits.

As Kris Macchiarola, author of *No Approval Needed*, told me in our podcast conversation:

"I know so many people who, behind the scenes, they're either miserable at work or they're miserable in their marriages. But if you look at their posts on social media, you would never know. We promote the fairy tale, the fantasy that we want everyone to see. Yet we're all more fascinated by the authentic, by the flaws, by the vulnerability. That is the part which makes us human and interesting. Yet, we often see that as weakness in ourselves, and we want to push it away. But that's what helps us to connect on a deeper level with other humans."

Indeed it does and, as such, it helps us LEAD better.

The better we connect, the better we can lead.

Reality resonates far more than perfection. Hence why vulnerability resonates so much more than the emotional distancing. The latter was so prevalent in old leadership methods. But today, leadership has changed, and leaders need to lean into those changes.

Thankfully, there are many inspirational leaders now speaking out about challenges, about vulnerable moments; mistakes they've made and struggles they've had. More and more, people are revealing that success doesn't come without failure and that challenges and difficulty have actually shaped those future successes and enlightened and strengthened people.

As Kris says, "It's our struggles and how we overcome them which makes the journey of achievement so much sweeter. If we didn't have the struggles, we'd care less."

Our own struggles and mistakes, the poor choices and decisions we make, are what teach us how to survive better. We learn how to do things right as a result of doing things wrong. So, when leaders share *how* they've got things wrong too – that's admirable and relatable and fosters a culture of trust and truth and growth –that cultivates the best kind of working environment in which people can truly thrive.

The Importance of Trust and Safety

"Become the kind of leader that people would follow voluntarily; even if you had no title or position."
Brian Tracy

Given a recent Engage for Success/Ashridge Executive Education/Oracle study which revealed that only a quarter of UK teams are fully engaged and giving their best at work, while *32% are actively disengaged, there's clearly a lot of work to be done.

From the study, researchers identified different zones of engagement, with the zone of disengagement including inward-looking teams, lots of cliques and high levels of mistrust, compared to the zone of engagement where teams are proactive and solution-focused. In the highly engaged zone, there's a positive atmosphere, a high degree of connectivity and team members support each other personally and professionally.

The report demonstrated the vital role played by leaders in engaging their workforce and stated 'having a team leader who is trusted and leads by example' as the most important factor, along with providing varied and challenging work and working with trusted colleagues.

Evidently, trust ranks highly in the engagement stakes.

And, given that trustworthiness is one of the first judgments people make on their first impression of you, we need to demonstrate our openness to those who come to work for us, the first time we meet them and from that moment onwards.

Amy Cuddy, Harvard professor and author of *'Presence'* has discovered a number of patterns in her 15year study of first impressions.

She says in her book that people's questions when they first meet you are:

Can I trust this person?
Can I respect this person?

These initial criteria are driven by an evaluation of a person's warmth and competence, respectively. And, while it's best to be perceived as having both, trustworthiness, or warmth, is the number one most important factor in how people judge you, rather than competence, which one might think would be judged as more important in a professional context. And yet the converse is true.

Trust and warmth matter more than respect and competence.

This makes sense given how, from an evolutionary perspective, it was a more urgent requirement to know how likely a fellow caveperson was to kill you or steal from you, than to know their fire-building competency. This is also why competence is only judged once trust has been established.

Hence why it's difficult to lead effectively and influence or even encourage people, if you're not trusted.

Old Leadership	vs	New Leadership
Power		Empower
Closed		Open
Guarded		Vulnerable
Competence first		Trustworthy first

"It's important to always create an environment where people feel safe to say what's on their mind," advises Leendert. "This creates more transparency. And if there's transparency, trust will come."

A common problem, however, is that companies find it difficult to foster that genuinely safe space for employees to speak up and be heard, perhaps because the primary connotations are that by putting their head above the parapet, they are going to get shot at.

So how do we foster this safe working space?

Stay Open

In her book, *Radical Candor*, Kim Scott relays a story about how she stood unnerved as her colleague Matt yelled at

Google Co-Founder Larry Page in a meeting where they were discussing each other's plans to fight Webspam. She feared his "vehement criticism" of the boss's plan might get him fired but Larry just grinned.

As Kim says, "he wanted not just Matt but everyone at Google to feel comfortable criticizing authority - especially his."

Indeed, being open to that led to more productive and collaborative discussions and permitted people to be themselves and fight their corner if they wholeheartedly believed or disbelieved in something.

What we can learn from this story is that good leadership involves, not just being open to showing your vulnerable side, but also being open to being wrong and inviting direct reports to feel at liberty to TELL you when you're wrong.

It's far better to be wrong and end up doing the right thing, than to let power and authority rule regardless, as was the old way of leadership.

When we open up the debate, we learn so much more.

Frankly, we want to hire people smart enough to tell us what to do and what not to do, rather than the other way around. But the only way to encourage that is to foster an open feedback culture, one built on autonomy and encouragement rather than control and micro-management.

Says Leendert, "It's not just about talking about creating a safe environment, it's about showing it through your actions, consistently showing it's okay to speak up, especially about the things that don't work. We have an operating principle as a management team, where we say, 'We challenge the professional, not the individual.' So, we challenge each other as much as we possibly can as professionals, but not as individuals. If we do the latter, the whole trust in what we're trying to achieve is gone."

Fiona McDonnell, Director of Consumer Retail at Amazon concurs. Says Fiona:
"Don't change who you are, but find the 'volume switch' on your leadership style so you can turn it up and down as needed to accommodate others."

Revealing our true opinions about a project or initiative, especially if we think those opinions may be unpopular, is part of leaning into our vulnerability. When we share in this way, we feel exposed and unsafe. Yet, ironically, when we voice our vulnerabilities and reveal our true selves, we get to feel safer.

This is something explored in *The Fearless Organisation: Creating Psychological Safety in the Workplace for Learning, Innovation, and Growth* by Professor Amy C Edmondson.

In the book, Professor Edmondson concurs that, in order to do their best work, people need to feel safe and secure in their working environment. She says the best way to create that safe environment is by developing a culture of open candour where opportunities to speak up are readily provided and every single individual feels they can express concerns and feel heard.

According to Professor Edmondson, "These are not things that happen routinely in most organisations, but they are mission critical to doing well in a complex, fast changing world".

An advocate of openness and candour, the author points out how "psychologically safe employees are more interested in learning, excellence, and genuinely connecting with others than in looking good".

This helps them let go of the need to cover and allows them to bring their best selves to work.

Says Amy, "Most organisations are hierarchical, but in some more than others, employees are acutely aware of status differences. In those organisations, people are overly careful and cautious around those higher up in the hierarchy."

For this reason it's important for leaders to:

- Remind people their input matters regularly. Tell them 'we need to know if we're doing something wrong.' We want you to tell us.

- Invite that input proactively and regularly. Ask specifically what people see in a certain situation and how you can help them out and what you could be doing differently.

- Respond with gratitude. Thank people for their feedback. Thank them for having the courage to speak up.

- Implement feedback or at least have further discussion about it, inviting the person with the feedback to be included in those discussions. That way, if their suggestions are not implemented, they can at least feel like they've contributed and see why and how the final decision has been reached, rather than feel like they've been ignored.

Creating a safe environment for people to voice concerns and offer negative feedback is only powerful when you either implement changes based on their feedback or keep them in the loop, rather than ignoring them and destroying trust.

And herein lies the missing link – for, in order to really hear what people are saying and to really grasp how people are feeling (or might feel if you respond in a certain way), you need another set of skills, you need emotional intelligence.

Chapter 4
Emotional Intelligence and Maturity

"D&I is about us all helping ourselves and each other to do well, so we can be better together,"
Susan Robson

What Makes A Good Leader? IQ + EQ + EM

Years ago, if I asked you to describe the key traits of a good leader, you'd no doubt have said, strength, passion, courage. You'd probably add that they need to be incisive, analytical, astute. And, of course, they need to have a decent level of intelligence. However, today, emotional intelligence (EQ) is as mission critical as IQ.

Today, to lead well, you need to be able to identify, understand and manage your own emotions and grasp how they relate to other people. But, even more than that, to really get to know, understand and empathise with each individual in your charge and to lead with service, as well as Emotional Intelligence (EQ) you need Emotional Maturity (EM) too.

So, what's the difference?

In a nutshell, 'Emotional Intelligence' is having the ability to accurately perceive, read and manage your own emotions and those of others; to understand what we feel and why and how these emotions can impact others, so we can readily express our own humanity in relation to those we work with.

Identifying, assessing and regulating emotions results in better management of our interpersonal relationships. Because, the better able we are at managing our emotional response to pressures and events and the potential emotional responses of the people we work with, the more able we are to build our capacity to connect deeply and communicate effectively.

As such, emotional intelligence isn't a soft skill, it's a strong skill - it's a powerful skill when it results in stronger connections.

And, let's face it, business can be emotional.

When we care about the work we do and are working with other people who also care in a mutual bid to succeed, we are likely to experience intense emotions; from frustration, worry, disappointment and even anger through to excitement, joy and fist-pumping celebration.

As such, having a good understanding of our own emotions and those of our team members is critical to help us to help them manage and cope accordingly and generate the best results.

Frankly, the better people feel the more productive and agile they are.

Meanwhile, Emotional Maturity (EM) is new concept derived from EQ which enables leaders to exercise EQ despite the existence of office politics, self-importance and an 'us vs them' mindset, which can easily creep into the leadership space.

The fact is, you might have a high level of Emotional Intelligence, but you may not actively deploy it, because of those restrictive factors listed above.

So, if you can suspend self-interest in favour of the success of others, you bring Emotional Maturity to the table. Equally, when you share your own vulnerabilities, despite it feeling outside of your comfort zone; when you focus on developing cultural competencies and building trust, despite the office politics and hierarchal systems around you, it's possible to demonstrate an Emotional Maturity which will serve you and those you work with incredibly well.

Yes, today's leaders – young, old, new and experienced, need to be generous and genuine in order to create teams of individuals who thrive and businesses which benefit from this deepened connection.

Why Emotional Intelligence Matters?

Of course, EQ isn't only about empathy and relationship building, it also helps with decision making and responding as effectively and rationally as possible to business hurdles. For when you understand the power of your emotions, you are more likely to notice when they are influencing a decision.

For example, say you've been right behind a strategy for some time but, having given it some careful consideration, you're sure it needs to be tweaked in order to work. Pride for your prior support of the project might influence you to keep going with it, despite your logic saying otherwise. EQ means knowing when to let your head rule over your heart and vice versa.

It can help you know ahead of time what the impact a core decision might have emotionally on your staff too, *i.e.* whether it might cause optimism or dismay and the knock-on effect of those emotions.

When you understand such impact, you're better equipped to form a strategy which will enable people to respond in a more measured way.

Additionally, EQ also helps you to notice the psychological wellness of individuals within your team, including your own state of mind, and can mean you're able to offer support and resources accordingly. (We'll discuss wellbeing in the workplace further in Chapter Six.)

Fundamentally though, the better you can understand people's responses, the better you can communicate with maximum clarity. For example, you have a firm grasp about what people do or don't find amusing or what does or doesn't motivate people, you can choose words which will best suit them and their personal foibles.

Coming back to that Maya Angelou quote about how you make people feel; as a decent leader, you want people to feel:

- Comfortable coming to you with any concerns or questions
- Receptive to your ideas and feedback, as well as demonstrate effectively that you are receptive to theirs
- Respected and validated. So that, should they disagree with you, they know you'll still respect their position and that any exchanges with you will be productive and intentionally respectful
- Supported and valued

When people feel the opposite of any of these things (undervalued, unsupported, disrespected or ignored), they also don't feel motivated to work with you or their team on accomplishing shared goals.

Making people feel how you want them to feel, to enable and empower them to do their best work under your leadership, takes EQ and EM.

The Five Pillars of Emotional Intelligence

So how do we go about best cultivating these skills?

Well, firstly, it's important to break down precisely what the core EQ competencies are, as defined by Daniel Goleman, the man who coined the Emotional Intelligence phrase in 1990:

Emotional Intelligence includes:

1. Self-awareness
2. Self-regulation
3. Motivation
4. Social skills
5. Empathy

1. Self-awareness

Self-awareness isn't just about knowing your strengths and weaknesses (although that's important too) it's also about knowing how you feel and how those emotions and actions can directly affect others.

2. Self-regulation
When you stay in control, you are better able to make logical rather than emotional decisions; you are better able to be

flexible rather than rigid. Leaders with strong self-regulation are also less likely to compromise other peoples' values or stereotype them.

3. Motivation
If you're going to motivate teams, you need to be able to motivate yourself too and work steadily towards your own goals in a way which inspires others.

4. Social skills
Good, open communication where you're as open to negative feedback as you are to positive feedback is vital, as is getting buy-in from individuals to support new projects and missions.

Social skills also lend themselves to resolving conflicts in a diplomatic way, and to demonstrating honest praise and encouragement.

5. Empathy
Being able to put yourself in another person's situation, to see something from their perspective, is a golden leadership skill. Because, when you understand how other people's feelings affect their behaviour and motivation, you can better communicate and connect with them to equip them with what they need to perform well.

Research reveals that leaders who show empathy receive consistently higher positive job performance ratings and enable those they lead to perform better too.

As Simon Sinek, author of *Leaders Eat Last*, suggests, empathy is the most vital tool in a leader's toolbox. It compounds positive relationships, helps leaders to get buy-in to a shared vision and enables them to lead their people towards their fullest potential.

Case Study: VaynerMedia

Gary Vaynerchuk, CEO of VaynerMedia is widely lauded as a leader who attributes his success to his high levels of self-awareness and empathy.

Having grown his father's wine business from $3 million to $60 million in five years with no marketing budget, Gary went on to co-found digital media agency, VaynerMedia with his brother AJ.

As Gary notes, "To build the company, I have to use the number one asset that I have: people and the relationships I have with them."

Over seven years, VaynerMedia has grown from a staff of 20 to 600 across five global offices.

Says Gary, "Caring about your employees doesn't just mean providing them with health benefits or 401(k) plans. When I say "I care about my employees," I really mean it. I'm passionate about knowing each and every one of them as individuals."

Gary cites 'trust' as the number one way to establish what motivates each individual in your business, which, he says, comes from acknowledging them as individuals.

"These interactions can be as small as a wink in the hallway or a wave as you walk past the conference room they're in," says Gary who recounts on his website how he calls this the 'Rickey Henderson Effect,' because, at Gary's first baseball game, Rickey Henderson caught a ball, winked at 10 year old Gary and, "for the next five years, I was his biggest fan."

Consequently, Gary has sat down for five minutes for a one-on-one with every new hire at VaynerMedia within a couple months of their recruitment, so he can find out how he might be able to help them achieve their goals.

When you make someone feel comfortable in your presence, they'll be open to coming to you if they're ever struggling or have something to discuss. Because they trust you.

However, Gary admitted that, despite this focus on "creating an environment where people were comfortable enough to approach the CEO with their internal issues", there was still only a sixth who genuinely do, "400 or so who are intrigued and want to buy-in, but are cynical because what we're trying to achieve is difficult' and the rest 'aren't their yet'. And that's why Gary created the Chief Heart Officer (CHO) position for Claude Silver.

My friend Dennis Ossipov-Grodsky who reports to Claude Silver told me during our podcast conversation that Claude had decided to leave VaynerMedia to focus on her passion of empowering leaders.

"But," explains Dennis, "Gary being Gary – he's very attuned – he brought her back and made her [the] second most important person in the company after himself."

"She's in charge of culture," says Dennis. "And when we announced her as Chief Heart Officer, the President of NASA called her and they had an hour and a half long conversation, exchanging notes."

Having one person who oversees anything to do with people is one of the best ways a leader can really show their commitment to those people's wellbeing in the company. And she's more than just Head of HR, she's in charge of enabling connection. And the only way to truly enable connection is to have a good level of Emotional Intelligence, especially empathy.

Said Claude, in an interview with Forbes: "I always start from a place of 'this person can do no wrong.' I always start from a place of unconditional empathy."

I had the pleasure of meeting Claude in person to record a podcast and, what struck me about her was her ability to convey empathy and connect so quickly on a deeper and more meaningful level. It was the first time I had met with Claude, yet I felt I had known her for years. Claude is an emotional optimist, coach, manager, and mentor. As the first ever Chief Heart Officer in VaynerMedia she feels honoured to work for 800 Humans where she describes being in touch with the heartbeat of every single person in the company. Her purpose, as she sees it, is to infuse the agency with empathy. She describes culture as a texture, a vibe and a feeling; something that is alive and definitely not one or two-dimensional, but three-dimensional.

"Culture is, in a nutshell, the heartbeat for me. It is something that absolutely lights up an entire system — if it is in place, and if it is thriving."
Claude Silver

Of course, we're not all naturally empathic, but we can all learn to be more so.

Especially given the wide-reaching role that today's leaders have in leading themselves, leading other people and leading their organisations. This takes a combination of those key five traits as defined by Daniel Goleman.

How To Cultivate Emotional Intelligence and Maturity

Self-Mastery

"Knowing others is intelligence; knowing yourself is true wisdom. Mastering others is strength; mastering yourself is true power."
Lao Tzu

Successful leaders need to be aware of their own imperfections, their strengths, weaknesses, their emotional triggers and their reactions. They need to learn from mistakes, use their strengths and delegate to fill gaps in their weaknesses. Once they've cultivated this high level of self-awareness and self-reflection, they can enable others to develop equally strong self-mastery and create a more open-minded and emotionally intelligent culture.

- Know who you are, what matters most to you and what values you hold dear. Then demonstrate integrity by sticking to those values.

- Reflect – take responsibility for how you respond and take time to reflect on whether you've responded according to your values and in a way in which you've wanted to respond.

- Journal – writing down thoughts will enable you to reflect on what you've thought, felt and done, what you've learned and how you might best proceed. Recording these reflections gives you the chance to notice patterns and reactions and tweak them if necessary.

- Commit to accepting being accountable for your actions. Lead by example in this way and share what you've learned with your team. Sharing your mistakes and what you've learned from them doesn't make you less respectable as a leader, it makes you more so, as it also makes you more relatable, more human and, crucially, more trustworthy. It also demonstrates good self-awareness and inspires others to hold themselves accountable and make progress through learning too.

- Practice using your breath to stay calm and teach others about the power of breath too. If you make your exhale slightly longer than your inhale, this has the power to relax you. Stress and anxiety prevent us from accessing the logical part of our brains because our 'fight or flight' response takes over. Literally the only way to regain access and rationalise is to calm ourselves down, and the best way to do this is to tune in to our breath and breathe slowly. We can also take action to do something which forces us to use the thinking part of our brain rather than the emotional part.

As Cheryl Rickman explains in *The Happiness Bible*, "Take three deep breaths, then try counting backward from 100 in sevens. Controlled breathing helps to lower our stress response, so that we can calm anxious thoughts. If you're still not calm, tap into your senses rather than your thoughts, by focusing on what you can hear, see and smell. When we calm ourselves, we can focus and regain control of our minds."

- Express yourself by writing down your negative feelings about a situation on a piece of paper and then ripping it up. This allows you to express, check and challenge your feelings without voicing them (and regretting doing so).

- Be optimistic and find the good. A positive mindset is motivational, especially when you're able to practice seeing the silver lining in the clouds which come in form of failure or other challenges. There's always a lesson to be learned somewhere and the more you can reflect on the good parts of a situation and communicate those with your team, the more optimistic everyone will be.

Leading Others

Leaders work with you, bosses instruct you. Indeed, as Henry Kissinger said, "Leadership is about taking people where they would not have got by themselves."

And to do *that*, you need to inspire and encourage people to be their best selves; enable them to trust in you and, vitally, you need to get to know where they want to go – where are you leading them, and does that tally with their own ambitions?

Meanwhile, to lead the organisation overall, leaders need to inspire with a clear vision and be able to articulate that vision and mission with clarity to all stakeholders – from boards and partners to clients and competitors alike. This requires the ability to connect well and build strong relationships.

- Invest time in meeting every single person at every level and function. In order to unlock the potential in every individual who works for you, you need to get to know them sufficiently and find out who they are and that takes time. Ask them:
  - What matters most to them?
  - What motivates them?
  - What are they seeking and striving for?
  - How can you help remove the obstacles in their path to help them reach what they seek?
  - What activities engage them and challenge them?
  - Where do they find flow in their working lives, where they lose track of time as they are so deeply engaged?
  - Where do they struggle?
  - What bores them and what excites them?
  - How do their values fit with the organisations? And how can you help them to express their own individual values within that wider context?

- What are their strengths and weaknesses?
- How do they really feel during their working day?
- How can you help them to feel better?

- **Give your people the opportunity to get to know each other.** As well as getting to know them all yourself, give each employee the chance to share their different stories with each other. Host events which enable this and celebrate individuality.

- **Personalise your introductions.** When introducing people to each other, personalise. Mention their strengths and what they might have in common. For example, 'This is Sheena, she's doing great things in the networking space. She's been here for 4 years now and she plays a mean game of tennis.' This demonstrates that you know them well.

- **Lead by example.** As we've explored, be open in sharing your own story and include the uncomfortable parts – your failures, mistakes and regrets as well as your hopes for the future. This humanises you and helps you connect better on a human level.

- **Read body language.** See if you can determine from this how people feel. Reflect on whether you were right or wrong and learn from the signals you picked up and those you missed.

- **Open up contribution at meetings to generate conversation and idea input**. Ensure everyone knows that meetings are meant to be places where diverse views and opinions are gathered and celebrated.

- **Provide opportunities to feedback and implement suggestions** (or discuss why suggestions aren't being implemented – include the person suggesting change in the discussions). This ensures people feel like they matter and belong, so keep this 2-way communication line open and consistent. Opportunities often come in the disguise of obstacles. The feedback you gain about what you're doing wrong could give you that opportunity to do something different and better. So we should welcome it, value it, and use it to grow.

- **Have humility**. Be thankful for all the feedback – the constructive, the critical, the formal and the informal – remember that defensiveness gets in the way of betterment.

- **Celebrate successful events and reward effectively.** Recognition is crucial in helping people feel valued.

- **Accompany every piece of negative feedback with five positive statements**. According to the Losada Ratio and our in-built negativity bias, human beings have a tendency to focus on the negative, so we need to balance this out with encouragement and notice what our people are doing right as much as what they are doing wrong.

- **Choose your words and how you use them wisely.** Care about what you say and how you say it so that people know that you meant what you said.

- **Listen and notice and ask.** Active listening one of the most important skills for leaders to develop. Rather than listening to reply, listen to understand. So, listen attentively. Look at the person who's speaking to you, maintain eye contact and pay attention to what people say. Ask the person to tell you more, so they feel genuinely heard and respected.

The more emotionally intelligent and mature we are as leaders, the more we can bring others along in developing their own EQ and EM skills.

Of course, in order to cultivate these skills and lead others well, there is one common factor we need to practice. We need to be leaders who listen well.

Active Listening

Only when we learn to really listen can we truly hear the multitude of voices and allow the multiplicity of each individual to shine – fully.

We can only empower diverse voices and foster inclusion and belonging when we position ourselves to truly HEAR those voices.

Leaders therefore need to be able to lead with considerate communication, because our response to what others say can have a positive or negative impact on how they feel.

But how do we communicate in a considerate way so that we may create a solid foundation for relationships to thrive and bolster connection?

The answer is to practice active listening and constructive response.

Research has shown that how we react to people's ideas and good news – whatever they are excited about sharing, dictates how good or bad our relationships with others are.

The four different responses are:

1. **Active Constructive Response**: Visually, this includes strong eye contact, nodding and smiling to demonstrate enthusiastic support and interest in what the person is saying. Orally, this includes questions that invite the person talking to tell you more and gives them the opportunity to relive the experience and maximise their enthusiasm in sharing, such as, 'How did that feel..?' or 'What happened next? What did they say after you'd said that?' or 'That's amazing, you must be so excited. Tell me more...'

2. **Passive Constructive Response**: Visually, this includes looking somewhere else, other than at the person sharing. Orally, this includes dismissive auto-pilot responses, such as 'Oh, that's nice' or 'Yeah?' This is one of the most common modes of response. We've all had it done to us, but we're probably as guilty of doing it to others.

3. **Active Destructive Response**: Visually, this includes frowns or quizzical looks. Orally, this includes

questioning and belittling the news with statements such as 'But won't you be more tired if you take on that project?' or 'Wouldn't you rather do such and such instead?' or 'Won't that create such and such a problem?'

4. **Passive Destructive Response**: Visually, this includes looking away and walking away, possibly having frowned or shaken your head first or smiling in a 'fake' way. Orally, this includes either silence (ignoring the other person completely) or shifting the focus back on to the supposed listener rather than the speaker. The person listening is listening to answer rather than to learn.

EXERCISE: Good Listener

Have team members get into groups of four and take it in turns to play the part of the sharer of good news and the listener.

How can the listener show their interest and encouragement and draw out the story so the speaker can relive their experience?

Can they use 'what', 'where', 'when', 'how' and 'why' questioning to draw out the news? And what might they do to the contrary?

Invite the two remaining group members to guess which of the four responses are being used.

Listening well fosters respect and develops trust. Conversely, listening poorly weakens relationships. If you listen intently, you'll learn more and find out something you didn't know before. But, even more critically, you'll enhance your relationship with that individual.

And everyone deserves to share their own story.

The Equality of Stories

Evidently how we listen and respond to people is critical to the depth of our connections and the health of our relationships. But it's also important from a D, I & B perspective because, it's about the equality of humanity – the equality of stories.

Like me, MD at Accenture, Andrew Pearce, was adopted by white parents and, as he says, "there are not many black people in the Lake District." Consequently, this led to him not knowing what he was going to be called at school from one day to the next. "It often depended what was on the TV at the time," says Andrew.

"But that fostered in me a need to show that actually you should not judge people on their gender, ethnicity, sexuality, or enablement. There should be no judge. People should be

allowed to be themselves, be authentic, not have to aspire or conform to this one medium, but to be their whole selves."

Andrew's mother fostered that into him – to always be proud of who you are and be yourself. But being different also fostered in Andrew that desire for equality and the knowledge that, as he says, "everybody has a story, and it's important that we listen to those stories!"

As Andrew puts it:
"We have two ears and one mouth for a reason. People tend to listen - not to understand, they listen because they want to reply. And when you want to have a conversation about ethnicity or race or what needs to change - people are very keen to reply in a defensive way, rather than listen and understand what you're saying about what it actually feels like to be an individual of colour in this environment."

As such, when it comes to stories about people's own individual experiences, it's so crucial to listen and to listen well.

When we do so, we get to serve. And that is the most effective way to lead – from a place of service.

"Leadership is not about being the best. Leadership is about making everyone else better."

Andrew concurs:

"It's not about me. It's about what I can do to shine a spotlight on other people. I'm a great believer that if the spotlight shines on you [as a leader], use it to shine on somebody else. Because the legacy isn't about me, it's about what you do to make a more diverse and inclusive workplace and society going forward for generations who are going to be the next leaders.

"Being present is so important," agrees VP Marketing of Nespresso, Davide Moro. "That's why I avoid multi-tasking. I know it's difficult, but I go to meetings and I don't put my phone on the table. Instead I encourage conversation, thinking that I want to learn something. If your mouth is open, you're not learning."

So many of the great people I've interviewed for my podcast have specified the importance of listening. Take Desiree Barnes, who served as communications and public engagement strategist for former US President, Barack Obama and now runs her own strategic communications consulting firm, BRKDN Strategies.

"People asked Oprah how she became so successful as an interviewer and she said by being a good listener," says Desiree.

"To be a great leader, manager, employee or student, you have to constantly feed your appetite for curiosity, to take notice of the things around you and really listen," she adds. "But don't just listen to what people are saying, listen to the things that people are not saying! That's often how you'll find the best way to contribute, to fill in the gaps and offer something new."

Fiona McDonnell, Director, Consumer Retail Amazon, is also in agreement:
"Good leadership starts with listening. You need hear what's there, but importantly hear or feel what isn't there? And take steps to encourage the missing contributions to ensure balance in conversations."

To listen in these ways, you need to give people your full attention. This means putting down the mobile phone, asking questions which demonstrate your interest, follow up down the line and always let people finish before jumping in.

Not only does listening in this way earn respect and build relationships, it empowers us as leaders with more knowledge and it helps us connect better.

So, to summarise:

- Let people speak. Don't cut them off or criticise their suggestions.
- Be fully present so you can notice what is being said but also what isn't.
- Practice active constructive response to encourage people to share.
- Invite all feedback, both good and bad and demonstrate you're listening by implementing

suggested changes or keeping people in the loop and involved in discussions when suggested changes aren't implemented.

When we scratch behind the surface we reveal so much more and we empower people to join us on our own journey. When we connect well with the people we work alongside, it's far more enjoyable to work towards a shared vision, for a common purpose.

As reported in GungHo!, to feel inspired, people's work must be valued and seen as important; they must be encouraged and cheered on and, they must have autonomy over their own contribution.

"A leader. . .is like a shepherd. He stays behind the flock, letting the most nimble go out ahead, whereupon the others follow, not realizing that all along they are being directed from behind."
Nelson Mandela, Long Walk to Freedom

Yet effective leadership is not perfect leadership. Some amazing people fail as leaders and some leaders who might not seem like they should be great leaders, just are.

This is because they build trust, develop empathy and cultivate connections.

But it's also because there is wind behind their sails.

And that wind is their why; that wind is their purpose.

Chapter 5
Purposeful Culture and Leadership

"Unless someone like you cares a whole awful lot, nothing is going to get better. It's not."
Dr Seuss

Business used to be seen as a realm where nobody cared. "It's just business," the cold-hearted expensive-suited business tycoon would say to justify his harsh decision or poor treatment of others. But, no longer.

Today, corporations need to care about more than their bottom line, they need to care about doing good; they need to stand for something bigger than profit – to have a purpose.

Behavioural science shows that, as humans, we all have a basic need to contribute to something bigger than ourselves. Purpose fulfils this need. Both our own inner purpose and that of the companies we work for. And if the two are aligned – that's a powerful match, which brings out the best in people and enables companies and their people to flourish.

Ultimately, human beings need meaning – that sense that our life has inherent value and significance, based on what we do and why we do it. When we go to work we need something to believe in and work towards that runs deeper than making money.

Money only serves the needs at the lower end of our hierarchy of needs, our physiological and safety needs, according to Abraham Maslow's 'Theory of Human Motivation'. Love and belonging come next, then our esteem and self-actualisation, to which our contribution to the world and purpose within it make an impact. Essentially, we need something that matters to us, which speaks to our values and to who we are as human beings.

Increasingly, this is true of the places we choose to work and also in relation to the products and services we buy too.

Purpose Power

There has long been a business case for purpose, ever since Jim Collins wrote about visionary companies which were *'Built To Last'* in 1994 and ever since Simon Sinek compelled us to *'Start With Why'* in 2009.

Businesses with a guiding purpose for what they do beyond profit are the ones which best appeal to consumers, investors and talent. They are the ones which commercially thrive as a consequence of doing good.

Consequently, leaders have realised that it matters less what their business does; it matters more *why* their business does it. Part of what made them realise is this is down to the key paradox of business - that those which are the most profitable are not those which are the most profit-focused. Rather, they tend to be those which are the most purpose-focused.

What Is Purpose and Why Has It Become So Critical?

As Kenja CEO, Ted Katagi wrote: "Purpose is your North Star, it is your unwavering unchanging goal which your daily actions will lead you to."

As individuals, we are spending more time figuring out our own true purpose to bring meaning to our working lives. Meanwhile, companies are doing the same.

An EY Beacon Institute sponsored Harvard Business Review Analytic Services (HBRAS) survey defines purpose as "an aspirational reason for being which inspires a call to action and provides benefit to local and global society."

This is a fine definition, for it encompasses everything that a purpose should be: inspirational, actionable and beneficial.

A strong purpose inspires and motivates, satisfies and clarifies.

It feeds strategy, branding and engagement, both of customers and employees.

It explains why you are pursuing your goals and is reflected in how you create and sell your products and services.

In achieving all of this, purpose outlives every campaign, strategy and project. It's the golden thread which runs through it all.

What's more, a definable purpose is measurable. Therefore, it is something which companies can make progress on.

Today though, purpose is no longer merely about CSR (Corporate Social Responsibility), it's no longer a box-ticking exercise, it's about a deeper and more radical sense of societal and employee engagement - a win-win for your business and for society at large.

Today purpose is the yin to profit's yang. And we're currently in the eye of the perfect storm for prioritising purpose in business because of a few key drivers. These include:

- A decline in how much people trust businesses and executives over the past decade has created a 'trust deficit'. Trust needs to be earned back and purpose is a key enabler in re-building this trust.
- Environmental issues and sustainability concerns around climate change and plastic pollution, among other issues, are top of global citizens' agenda. Sufficiently so that companies of all sizes must be responsible about their environmental impact in terms of how they produce, supply, package and consume. Supply chains are coming under public and regulatory scrutiny more than ever before. Meanwhile, the 'Triple Bottom Line' has become increasingly important as

customers' expectations over the social and environmental responsibilities of big business have risen exponentially over the past few years.

- Pay gaps between employees and executives and between genders are timely topics which need addressing. Social inequality has been exposed and only serves to decrease morale and increase bitterness around businesses which continue to pay unfairly.

- The rise in social media empowering the public to voice their views on brands has made the requirement to do good even more paramount. Customers can express their opinions at will and destroy brand reputations in seconds. Consequently, businesses today are held accountable for their actions. So having a purposeful goal to align actions with is a useful guide.

Why The Business of Doing Good Is Good For Business?

It makes sense to prioritise purpose, not just environmentally or socially, but commercially too. Harvard professors have proven over the past decade that purposeful values-driven companies have outperformed their counterparts in stock price by a factor of 12. But that's not all.

People like to contribute to a good cause, whether that's through working for or buying from companies which serve those causes.

But why else is "the why" so critical in the modern business landscape?

The bottom line is, companies which have a clear purpose outperform those which don't – they generate more revenue, attract and retain more talent, keep that talent engaged and have more loyal customers. They also both manage change and innovate better.

Cultivating a purposeful culture is imperative because purpose:

1. **Builds trust and improves customer and stakeholder relationships.** Businesses now operate in a 'reputation economy' and this customer expectation of companies 'doing good' rather than merely 'not being bad' or 'doing less harm' is here to stay.
   Consumers and employees are wise to companies that say they are doing good yet which fail to prove it. Nowadays it's easier for customers to share their dissatisfaction and those customers crave transparency. With mistrust of Corporations, Government and Media growing rapidly in recent years, anything your business can do to build trust is golden.

   Customers will readily define how successful a company is in pursuing and achieving their purpose via the feedback they perpetually provide. So having a clear purpose serves an extra purpose of keeping a company customer-focused. And, as we know, the best way to sustain success in business is to sustain customer satisfaction. Without that, growth is a pipedream.

2. **Attracts and retains talent.** Employees and teams need something to believe in. It's now more widely known, from a well-being perspective, that contributing to something greater than ourselves matters as much as the money we're paid. Deloitte Millennial surveys consistently demonstrate that the majority of Millennials want to work for purposeful companies, so companies prioritising purpose find it easier to recruit and retain the pick of the best talent.

3. **Fuels innovation and improves team and financial performance.** This is because employees are more engaged and motivated to put in more effort when they are contributing to a wider purpose. When teams and individuals are positioned as problem-solvers with a common goal and vision they innovate well. BursonMarsteller and Business School IMD state that teams working for purposeful brands perform 17% better. Other reports show Unilever Sustainable Living brands performed twice as well as their other less purposeful brands.

4. **Improves decision making and buy-in**. A company's "why" is the emotional component, and, as such, the heart-winning component. Why a company does

something is a more powerful attractor (to attract customers, strategic alliance partners and talent) than 'what' they do, because we use our limbic brain to make decisions based on 'why' rather than the rational brain, which we use to make decisions based on "what." The latter causes over-thinking and analysis paralysis; the former captures our hearts and minds and leads us to make more instinctive decisions which are aligned with who we are as people and as organisations.

5. **Aligns suppliers and cultivates strategic alliances.** Common ground in each company's purpose can spark collaborative partnerships which are truly aligned. You can collaborate using your shared purposeful aim as the unifying common denominator. This goes for cross-departmental alliances within the same organisation too. Purpose essentially spells out what matters most to you and acts as a uniting guiding force.

6. **Provides a torch light during darker times.** As a leader facing a plethora of pressures from shareholder demands, market shifts, industry disruption and public scrutiny, purpose can be grounding. It's the still, solid axis in the centre of a constantly revolving wheel. This means that, during transformational times where market uncertainty and disruption dictates big changes, there is another constant other than change itself – purpose.

So, while change is constant, so too is purpose. This provides balance, a guiding light and an antidote to the fear prevalent in organisations during uncertain times. This helps people grasp the need for sometimes difficult purpose-led changes which will inform longer-term strategy. Purpose can therefore be comforting during times of change and it can spark action where inertia could have taken hold.

Together, these combined benefits of having a purpose makes it easier for companies to expand geographically, execute mergers and acquisitions with/of companies which share their purpose, engage in change and launch new products and services.

When you steer your ship with purpose, it's easier to guide it round obstacles and reach your destination. The same is true when people live their lives and steer their careers with a central aim guiding them. Purpose helps us not to 'sweat the small stuff', because none of that matters as much as the purpose we're pursuing and the intention we're working with.

However, just as a ship needs a good captain, companies need good leaders to drive the purpose operationally.

Breathing Life into Purpose

Of course, purpose is merely aspirational rhetoric unless it has measures and methods with which to progress it and make it tangible.

As such, intention must align with execution.

Not only do products and services need to satisfy customers, they must adhere to the pursuit of the company's purpose. And this requires measurement.

Meanwhile, purpose needs to be more than just words in an e-mail to 'all staff' or clever copy on marketing collateral, it needs to go beyond that into the heart and soul of the organisation.

Today, a company's purpose should feed every key aspect of the company: aims, brand, strategy and culture.

How Leaders Can Command a Purposeful Culture

"Culture eats strategy for breakfast" is a well-known sound-bite at business events. And, like all clichés, it's true. A business without the right culture will struggle to engage employees, drive productivity and will fall short of the results required to grow. Strategy comes *after* the establishment of culture and, these days, a culture must be a purposeful one.

The culture of the business is absolutely paramount because this is the environment and vibe which holds the team together and it should therefore be informed by purpose and policy.

The best working cultures are those which are inclusive, foster a sense of belonging, encourage participation, cultivate innovation and are driven by a common purposeful vision. It's so much easier to implement a sustainable business strategy once the purpose and culture are set.

This bigger picture directs the business and maps out its course; it's purposeful pathway. In this way a purposeful vision brings the people who work within it on a journey together and that journey is made all the more achievable and enjoyable because the destination is sufficiently clear that everyone knows where they are headed.

Conversely, if you don't know where the top of the mountain is, it's going to be very difficult to reach it.

That said, you don't need to have a completely plotted out and navigated route to get up the mountain – there are often multiple different routes and strategies to reach the summit. And all good businesses have the capacity for flexibility so they may pivot if necessary.

That's why purpose and culture eat strategy for breakfast, because they enable that flexibility and hold everything in place. They are the bright shining star atop the mountain, guiding the way forward as the business progresses purposefully onward.

And, when changes and transformations are required, the clarity of purpose can guide people through those changes more readily.

Only when leaders are able to clearly communicate and reinforce the purpose of the business, focus on the horizon and inspire a culture around that purposeful vision can they command leadership, rather than demand it.

Embedding purpose into your brand and your culture takes more than just stating your intentions, you need to bring it to life through the commercial activities you undertake.
It's not just a strapline or campaign to include in outward bound PR; purpose needs to be integrated into decisions, behaviours and embedded into the culture. As such, it should guide how you work with partners, peers, customers and staff.

As such, in order to embed purpose into a business, it's important for there to be:

- Authentic servant leadership, where promises to staff, customers and all stakeholders are kept and purpose and associated values are regularly and consistently communicated. Servant leadership is about serving a purpose and serving that first and foremost. It therefore puts purpose and service as a priority. Leaders should be seen to be checking whether decisions, projects, communications and so on are aligned to the overarching purpose of the company. With this in mind, leaders should ask:

  - Will this decision best serve the stakeholders in the business?

- o Will this decision best serve our purpose as a company; our *raison d'être*?

- Continuous focus on product and service development which solves problems and make a positive impact. Purpose can empower employees every single day to solve problems and determine the value-add. In this way, purpose can consistently drive innovation, market response and disruption.

- Policies established and behaviours recognised which fit with the values and purpose of the business.

- Strategies to continuously engage, reward and get the best from each person.

- Day to day planning, strategic actions and commercial decisions should be made with the purpose in mind - from supplier criteria to partnership choices. Purpose helps provide clarity on strategy and drive long-term focus rather than short-term results. It also helps you to set clear boundaries about what you will and won't do strategically to grow the business.

- Measurement: Regular reviews of commercial practices carried out to ensure multi-department pursuit of purpose; consistently asking how are we living our purpose to make a difference?

- Purposeful recruitment: Hiring people who are aligned with and committed to the core purpose of the business.

Inspiration Leads to Motivation

With purpose as a key driver, rather than merely hire people who meet qualification and experience requirements, business leaders are enabled to hire people who believe what they believe in; people with shared values; people whose own personal sense of purpose fits with that of the company.

And when you hire people who believe what you believe; who share your belief in what the right thing to do is, these people not only feel like they belong, but they are motivated to work hard and maximise their efforts to help you achieve your mission. A common purpose is a powerful motivator. What's more, people who share your purpose want to stay with your company to help you do it.

Of course, there's more to employee engagement than purpose, as we've explored in the preceding chapters on belonging and inclusion. But purpose is an important part of employee satisfaction in the modern world of work.

Once you've hired people who belong within the purposeful culture you've created, you can use your purpose to inspire them.

As Simon Sinek says, *"There are leaders and there are those who lead. Leaders hold a position of power or influence. Those who lead inspire us."*

And, the best way to inspire others is to paint a picture of a desired future which they believe in, buy into and want to help you arrive at.

The alternative to inspiration is manipulation and that only leads to fear rather than trust and can lead people to look for alternative employment, which gives them more than you can offer. Yes, you can attract and poach the best talent with the promise of a fat paycheque but they won't do their best work for you, because they haven't been inspired to follow you, rather money has been the manipulator.

Purpose-led individuals share a sense of camaraderie that you can only build if you have a clear and common purpose. They have a rocket-fuelled drive that you can only generate if those people feel motivated to work towards a common goal.

Because purpose energises staff and encourages them to innovate.

So how do you uncover your true purpose – both as a company and as an individual?

Uncovering Purpose: What's Your Guiding North Star?

Let's start with companies:

Establishing Your Company's Purpose

Apple do what they do because they 'think differently' and want to 'challenge the status quo'. As consumers we want them to keep doing that and those who work for them believe in and share that ethos.

Tesla aims to 'accelerate the advent of sustainable transport' while TOMS aims to make life better for children in need and literally donates a pair of shoes to a child in need with every single purchase. Each of these companies makes business decisions based on that golden thread of purpose which runs through everything they do. Their 'why' drives everything.

Whether you already know your purpose or whether your business needs to upgrade its current purpose to improve values-alignment, these questions will help.

Ask yourself:

- Why does your business do what it does (apart from to generate profit)?
- What do you help people do?
- How do you make people's lives easier or better?
- What do you aim to achieve in terms of making the world a better place?
- What societal challenges can you solve? What positive impact (social/economic/environment) do you strive to have?
- What bold changes do you want to see in the world and what role can your business have in those improvements?
- How might you alleviate problems by providing market solutions that you have competency to build?
- How much of a difference do you make and can you make to the world?
- What's your social value?
- What messages can you use your reach to spread?

- Perhaps you want to reduce poverty, develop community unity, spread wellbeing, improve citizens' health?

Whatever your company's purpose is, it needs to influence business decisions, inspire employees to work for you and customers to buy from you.
Your purpose might be to revolutionise the way something is done – the way people hire, the way companies collaborate, the way people build brands, attract customers, store goods, streamline accounting practices, and so on.

Write your statement of intention here:

We _____ so _____ .

We make a difference by_____ .

The purpose of large corporations may be different to the purpose of smaller companies because, for the smaller organisations, the life experiences of the founders frequently dictate their 'why': both the purpose of the companies they establish and their own inner purpose which guides their careers.

So, whether you're an entrepreneur founding and leading your own business or an intrapreneur who's paid to direct and manage another business, you can bring your own individual purpose to your role. And, in doing so you'll be able to lead with purpose.

That's certainly been the case for myself and those I've interviewed in my podcast.

Indeed, the main reason we, as individuals and business leaders start with 'why' is because we cannot avoid doing so. For us, our purpose or 'why' guides us, because it is the right thing to do and because our life experiences have made us want to prove ourselves and improve the lives of others. We strive to serve.

Life Experiences Shape Our Inner Individual Purpose

In 1963, Victor Frankl, author of *Man's Search for Meaning* wrote that, when people live their lives with a central purpose to build meaning around, they function at their best.

During his time as a Nazi concentration-camp prisoner, Frankl noted that those fellow prisoners who had a sense of purpose were more likely to survive than those who didn't. The latter gave up, whereas those who had a purpose to live for, something to look forward to and thus meaning to their lives, had hope and survived.

He noted that, even when life became unbearable, purpose made their lives worthwhile enough to keep going. Consequently, after the war, Frankl responded to this experience by using his life to serve others. This service, based on his own life experience, became his own purpose.

This is how to create the most authentic guiding purpose, by taking our own experiences and using them to determine how we wish to serve others.

Take Andrew Pearce, for example. After 16 years in the Air Force, Andrew Pearce is now MD at Accenture, Executive Sponsor of the Accenture African and Caribbean network and UK Chair of the ELC.

As a black baby adopted by white parents, Andrew had witnessed first-hand how his parents had to deal with daily judgements. He then went on to witness racism and sexism in the corporate world and developed a complete lack of judgement regarding race, gender and sexuality as a result. He has overcome racism and confirmation bias during his career through always over-delivering and encouraging others to treat people as individuals. And that response to his own early experiences has informed his purpose.

Today his purpose is to make a difference in the D&I space so that he may persuade people to avoid treating it as a mere box ticking exercise and so that he can speak up for the marginalised.

Andrew recalls when he heard disturbing language in the workplace he knew he had to speak up. "I thought, 'this isn't right'", remembers Andrew, who felt nervous at first, but took courage from knowing he wasn't the one in the wrong. "I knew I needed to speak up," says Andrew. "If I didn't speak up, I'd be complicit," he nods. "I couldn't be complicit in a world where people get left behind because of race or because of gender, or because of sexuality. I don't want to be complicit in that."

And so, Andrew spoke up and he's been speaking up for the rights of others ever since.

"It was the right thing to do from a moral standpoint," says Andrew. And that's how inner purposes are often formed – via our own values and moral compass. That's how people with a certain set of values come to work for companies which share those values and have a common purpose.

Susan Robson was also driven by the injustice in the workplace to do the work she does. Following eight years in PwC Management Consultancy, Susan currently works in the Internal Consultancy team at National Grid as a Principal Consultant and leads Women in National Grid, a gender diversity employee resource group, which promotes the professional development of women and works to attract and create a network of talent that will enable National Grid to deliver its strategic priorities.

She noticed the data, the 'pain points' and the unfairness of women being left behind. "If you can address those pain points, that, for me, is an even bigger driver than passion. It's the right thing to do, so I'm bought in with the heart's argument and also very much the mind argument too."

Whether your purpose has been shaped by your own personal experience and your heart or your mind's logical response to injustice and your inbuilt moral compass to do the right thing – purpose so often comes down to values and doing work which is satisfying and impactful.

> *"[S]He who has a why to live for, can bear with almost any how."*
> **Friedrich Nietzsche, German philosopher**

For me, as soon as I took ownership of my difference and saw it as a strength rather than the weakness I had, for so long, wanted to hide and mask, I knew what my purpose in life would be – to help other people to see their own differences as a strength; to empower others to recognise they have a voice which is equally worthwhile and to inspire and encourage a new generation of leaders with a shared purpose of wanting to make a positive difference in the world.

Our new purpose lead organisation, DIAL Global, stands for Diverse Inclusive Aspirational Leaders (www.dialglobal.org).

Our Vision is
One where every individual is treated as an equal.

Our Passion is
Inspiring, educating and motivating others to make our world a better place, now and for future generations of leaders.

Our Mission is
To put purpose before profit and to win hearts and minds through purpose and action resulting in positive and meaningful change

Our Actions are
Delivering impactful experiences though our bespoke workshops, exclusive events, and our digital media and global engagement platform. Delivering an end to end engagement experience with multifaceted integrated learning, development and engagement solutions driven by the world's most innovative companies and thought leaders.

Ever since I replaced my initial purpose of making money with ensuring everything I do aligns with these central intentional aims, I have witnessed a huge difference in the good I am able to do and the rewards for doing so.

I truly believe in the power of sparking conversations and ideas to make our world a better place, now and for future generations of leaders, which is why my business campaigns for the power of knowledge and education from the worlds thought-leaders and inspired thinkers. As a result, we're building a global community of inquisitive individuals who are keen to engage with ideas from each other, both online and at DIAL GLOBAL events around the world. We also believe in putting purpose and passion before profit, so pledge to give a portion of our profits back to charity.

So, just as purpose can be the constant axis in the centre of a fast spinning wheel for corporations, this is true of individual purpose. This has been true for Andrew and myself and also for others I've had the good fortune to meet and interview.

Certainly for Desiree Barnes, that has been the case. She's gone from trainee doctor to serving as Communications and Public Engagement Strategist for former US President, Barack Obama to founding her own strategic communications consultancy for contemporary artists and scaling start-ups, BRKDN Strategies. But her purpose has always been to serve people in helping them to communicate the messages they want to put out into the world.

She started on her career with a scholarship to learn medicine as she "didn't want to feel disenfranchised anymore." It was only when one of her college deans told her that she didn't advocate for herself enough that, with the big things she wanted to do she needed to speak up and pursue what she wanted, that Desiree realised she wasn't pursuing her true purpose in life. She had only gone into medicine to prove that she could. Says Desiree, "I wasn't passionate about medicine but I was passionate about people."

This people-led purpose led her to pivot and apply for an internship with the Obama Fellowship.

"I knew that I understood people, I could communicate with people and have conversations with them. Field organising for any type of politician starts with one-to-one conversations. And when people fell in love with Barack Obama's story, which he was adamant should be a collective narrative about a collective voice, he spoke for and told the story of hardworking Americans everywhere, and having the courage to share that - is what made America resilient and great."

So Desiree's dream took shape in a different form. During her decade long tenure with the Obamas, she was a member of the communications team - where she oversaw daily operations and message execution as adviser to the press secretary, Josh Earnest. Concluding the administration, Desiree joined the personal office of Obamas to craft post presidency messaging and public engagement.

Then, after leaving the Obamas, she let her purpose steer her towards helping people communicate again. This time, by founding her own strategic communications firm to help the creative people from the neighbourhoods where she grew up. In doing so, her purpose has taken Desiree full circle.

The same is true of Paul Sesay, who now runs the Inclusive Top 50 UK Employer benchmark and the National Diversity Awards. Why? Because he didn't have the answer to the question, "who's the most inclusive employer in the UK?"

And, being a naturally inquisitive person, he wanted that answer, so he resolved to find out.

It was Paul's own life experience which led him to want to give back. Having grown up in foster care in the notably racist 1970s/1980s Leeds and Liverpool, he was greatly encouraged and supported by various role models and organisations in his youth. These helped him to believe in himself and pass his GCSEs. Consequently, Paul wanted to contribute to make a difference to those who would follow him. As a result, Paul's 'why' is to cultivate real change in society; to benchmark D&I for organisations and provide support and consultancy for companies who need help improving their own D&I. Ultimately Paul wants to enable organisations to better reach into communities and, in doing so, cultivate a win-win for businesses tapping into those harder to reach communities and for the individual talent within them.

For Paul, Andrew, Susan, Desiree and so many of the people who've featured on my podcast, our difference gave us a sense of purpose, not only to prove ourselves, but to speak up for others, from the disenfranchised minorities to the former President of America.

Each of us wants to see a real change in society and with that being the case, we needed to be the change. We couldn't be complicit, we had to be outspoken and follow our true purpose in life. Only then could we begin to make a real difference.

Championing D&I and inspiring young leaders has become the central aim of us all. What we do and how we do it are different, but our why is very similar. And when people with shared 'whys' get together, pull resources and collaborate, that's when big change can really happen.

That's what Sharon Amesu is finding. Now chair of the IOD in Manchester, Sharon was the first female woman of colour in a chair role at the IOD. She shows such strength of character and really embraces "Servant leadership". I am lucky enough to sit on her committee, where I head up Diversity and Inclusion. At a time where the IOD has suffered at the hands of bad press and racist remarks from the former London Chair, Sharon took this role on at a really momentous time and strives to make a true difference. That is made all the more possible because she is uniting and collaborating with people who share her vision for the future and purpose for the IOD.

As soon as she took on the role, Sharon built a new committee with people from diverse and unique walks of life. From 21-year-old tech entrepreneurs to seasoned management professionals, the committee has been given a breath of fresh air since she joined. Now she's busying herself with transforming the business from a stuffy "old boys' club" to an inspiring, fresh faced membership organisation which embraces leaders from all walks of life.

Sharon is a shining example of how your 'why' and your purpose in life can be a golden thread running through the middle of whatever you do, no matter how different those roles might be.

Growing up near Moss Side during the civil unrest of the 1970s and 1980s, ever since her dad's social activism work, which concerned bringing together West Indian parents whose children were facing racial discrimination within the education system, Sharon always knew she wanted to speak up for people and help them live better lives.

That led her to become one of the first female criminal barristers of colour in the country. As she explained in our podcast conversation, "I wanted to use my voice in the way which I'd seen my dad do, to represent those who felt disempowered; to advocate on their behalf and speak to those injustices in society. I had that clear intention that I wanted to use my voice to speak out for those who felt disenchanted by the system."

Sharon did so for 16 years. However, she became increasingly frustrated as, despite a focus on domestic abuse work, she found that she wasn't able to pursue her purpose of empowering and enabling those without a voice as much as she'd hoped. She consistently found, when women would finally report the abuse, by the time they saw Sharon they'd grown disenchanted with the whole process and no longer wanted to pursue the case for varying reasons, but she knew it was in the public interest to do so. Of course, it didn't sit well with her to force women to testify, so she started to wonder how else she could pursue her purpose of working in a space which would be about empowering and enabling people.

"That sense of frustration coincided with me being introduced to coaching," explains Sharon. And it was coaching which helped Sharon continue with her own people-led purpose.

Serendipitously, a decade ago, Sharon happened upon a coaching circle of women while she was trying to find a guitar class. She'd spent most of the class searching for the room in which the guitar lessons were being taught, being directed towards various empty rooms so when she arrived in the room of guitar-less women 45 minutes late for the guitar lesson, they invited her in. She was so inspired by the programme, she stayed on it for the next seven weeks. "My life was completely transformed," smiles Sharon.

"I loved asking myself searching questions, and asking other people searching questions about me. That self-awareness about my values and uncovering what I really wanted to do in the world to make a difference was so empowering."

So much so that Sharon decided this was what she wanted to do for other people, and off she went on her purposeful journey training to become a coach.

Despite her career change, this central thread of purpose remained – helping people to put right what was bothering them with the additional thread of helping others bring their own purpose to the surface.

Whereas before she'd focused on speaking up for other people; being their voice, now she could empower them to speak for themselves; to find their own voice and uncover who they truly were and wanted to show up in the world.

These days, as well as Chair of the IoD Manchester, Sharon is an award-winning Professional Speaker and Leadership Communication Specialist and has taken her 16 years at the Criminal Bar to challenge businesses to 'Raise the Bar' on their Leadership Communication. She's also a Leadership Fellow of St George's House, Windsor Castle and one of only four appointed Leadership Facilitators for the Leadership Programmes run at St George's House.

"We are the product of our environment, of our upbringing, of what we've been exposed to and that's very much shaped who I am, what I believe, what I aspire to do, and the impact I want to make in the world," says Sharon.

Today Sharon is continuing that purpose of empowering others in the work she's currently doing with the Institute of Directors as Chair. One of the key areas of focus for her there is D&I and social mobility.

Sharon explains:
"I believe business has a part to play in enabling that whole justice piece in society. So it very much shapes the way I think, the connections I see, and the gaps I see in society. These are

very much forged by my experiences growing up as a young child, and then into my early career at the Bar."

When it was suggested that she get into the world of professional speaking, Sharon felt 'imposter syndrome' rise within her and said that she didn't know how to do that. But it was pointed out that she'd been doing that for the first 16 years of her career. "Oh no, I was really just persuading a jury," she responded. But then she realised that *was* public speaking in itself, and she joined The Professional Speaking Association.

Now, Sharon speaks at conferences and organisations around courageous conversations and leading through change; still empowering others, but now she's speaking to them as well as speaking up for them in her IOD role – a combination of roles, which all have her core purpose – of empowering people – at their heart.

The same can be said of Alexandra Watson, best-selling author of *The Happiness System* and editor-in-chief of *SHINE* Magazine, who was one of the first female coaches in the country.

Her passion is about the advancement of women and so that is her core purpose. Everything she does is about the advancement of women – the magazine she publishes, the speeches she gives and the leadership training for women that she now provides.

"Wanting to really advance women by giving them the tools they need to get out of their own way and to surpass the limitations of society and the culture, is what drives my working days."

So what do *you* love to do, Dear Reader?

EXERCISE: Purpose

Defining your own purpose as a leader and inviting your team members as individuals to define theirs too can be a useful exercise, especially when tied in to the company-wide and wider-team purpose. It can enable you and other participants to see how your contribution at work not only helps you to fulfil the company's purpose, but enables you to pursue your own personal purpose too, giving your working lives more meaning – one of the core pillars of wellbeing.

Ask participants (including yourself) to consider and define their core purpose, values and mission by asking them to answer the following questions:

- Which causes matter most to you? What do you care about the most?
- What makes you feel angry and want to take action?
- If you were able to wave a magic wand to put things right, what changes would you make to society?
- What values would you/do you want to instil in your children?
- How would you wish to be remembered by others?

- What are you particularly good at and passionate about doing?
- How might you use your passion and skills to influence positive change around issues you care most about?
- How can you align your values, issues that matter most to you and your strengths to do purposeful work for your company?

As well as purpose being something you feel so strongly about that you cannot not do it – an unmistakeable 'why' which will likely have been shaped by your own personal experiences and your 'story so far' – it's also going to be helpful if you enjoy what you do and if you use your own unique set of character strengths and skills in order to achieve your purpose goals.

For, when you mix your purpose with your strengths you not only work purposefully to make the world a better place, you also boost your wellbeing at work. And, as a leader, the better you feel at work, the more able you are to help others feel good too.

Chapter 6 - Wellbeing – Cultivating a Happy and Engaged Workforce

"Happiness defined by you, must be the North Star of our society –
not stuff or bank accounts."
Gary Vaynerchuk

We spend the majority of our days at work. In fact, we spend more time at work than we do with loved ones.

So work should be a place that everyone feels good about coming to.

According to a Mental Health Foundation report, "the value added to the economy by people who are at work and have or have had mental health problems is as high £225 billion per year of value to the economy, which represents 12.1% of the UK's total GDP." As such, it's important that, as business leaders, we do all we can to help people feel good in the workplace.

In recent years there's been a lot of publicity about wellbeing and making workplaces fun and welcoming. But there's a lot more to wellbeing at work than free fruit, nap pods and 'wellbeing weeks', as we'll explore in this chapter.

Because everyone deserves to be happy at work.

Good leaders want to do good. Our "why" is often to make the world a better place in some way. And that's commendable but, if we wish to "do no harm" and "do good" instead, we should ensure our place of work does those who work for us no harm. Wellbeing is more than a health and safety issue. We should aim to help our people feel good.

Essentially, the way to keep hold of good people is to keep them happy, keep them secure and sufficiently reward and engage them.

"Take care of your employees and they will take care of your business. It's as simple as that."
Sir Richard Branson

As we have explored throughout this book, everyone wants to feel understood and cared for; to feel like they have a voice that is listened to. People want to feel seen, heard and appreciated. Caring about their wellbeing feeds into those basic human needs, but also helps them feel supported, even nourished. When you show your people that you are prepared to invest in their wellbeing you appeal to a higher level of trust. Showing you care is highly motivational.

In fact, in recent studies, the level of interest from management in an individual's level of well-being is said to be the most engaging and motivating factor of all, even above pay or career development.

Well-treated staff treat customers well and work better for the business (and stay working for the business). Showing you care about their well-being also leads to a reduction in the number of days taken off, reducing downtime and sick pay.

Why Wellbeing Matters

"The link between wellbeing and productivity is undeniable and calculable. It cannot be ignored."
Lawrence Waterman OBE

The statistics are well-known: a happy workforce equates to a productive one. And the more people feel happy and supported in their roles, the more likely they are to stay with a company.

So, strong levels of wellbeing positively impact both the bottom line and staff retention, which means higher company revenue and lower turnover of staff.

As well as improving performance and productivity, high levels of staff and leader wellbeing reduce absenteeism and health costs, improve corporate image, help attract and retain talent and improve the culture of a company.

And it's a two-way street: work impacts wellbeing and wellbeing impacts work. So, just as wellbeing is important at work, so is work important to our wellbeing. A recent YouGov survey commissioned by Business in the Community revealed three in five employees had experienced mental health issues *because* of work. Good leaders need to therefore do all they can to ensure work doesn't contribute to illness, but to wellness.

Work related stress and a lack of balance can trigger or exacerbate mental illness, such as anxiety and depression. Presentations, deadlines, interviews, appointments can all cause anxiety and overwhelm, just as having too little to do and monotony can be equally challenging.

And, given the alarming statistics around levels of employee engagement in today's workplaces, there's never been a more important time to care, both from a human perspective and a commercial one. Indeed, with employee engagement levels low and stress levels high, it's a critical time for leaders to care about how their people feel in the workplace.

And yet, a paradox exists around wellbeing in the business space. For, while a BUPA survey of 500 SMEs revealed 76% of SME leaders admitted the significant impact on growth of long-term sickness absence of a worker, only 46% prioritised health and wellbeing as 'a key consideration' with 43% stating they will 'never consider providing health and wellbeing benefits'.

This may have been partially in their considering such benefits to include more traditional offerings, such as health insurance. But BUPA says it was also, in part, due to the perception that companies with between 40-100 workers do not consider themselves large enough to prioritise employee health and wellbeing. And yet, the consequence of this dismissive attitude can result in lost talent, market share and custom as their best people leave to join more supportive competitors who *do* prioritise wellbeing.

It's vital for leaders to devote energy to sustaining the wellbeing of their staff as well as tending to their own wellbeing. Self-care and staff-care are equally important when it comes to leadership. Especially given the inevitable highs and lows of being an entrepreneur and/or business leader.

But first, before we explore the interventions leaders can put in place to prove they care, help people feel good at work, while also looking after themselves, let's define wellbeing.

What Does Wellbeing at Work Actually Mean?

We've come a long way since the birth of occupational health in 1700, when Bernardino Ramazzini first suggested doctors ask the occupation of their patients. Exposure to noise pollution, hazardous dusts and other ill-health causing irritants has been controlled, but nowadays long work hours and other stress-inducing factors, such as the uncertainty of job insecurity, have come to the fore. Today we need to consider a whole lot more.

Yet wellbeing is not merely about the absence of mental illness. Nor is it just about life satisfaction or, in a work setting, job satisfaction. The British Safety Council defines wellbeing as "a description of an individual's ongoing state which enables a person to thrive or not".

Meanwhile, The World Health Organisation defines workplace wellbeing as "a state where every individual realises his or her own potential, can cope with the normal stresses of life, can work productively and fruitfully, and is able to make a contribution to her or his community".

The National Institute for Health and Care Excellence (NICE) states that "health relates to a person's physical and mental condition. Wellbeing is the subjective state of being healthy, happy, contented, comfortable and satisfied with one's quality of life. Mental wellbeing relates to a person's emotional and psychological wellbeing. This includes self-esteem and the ability to socialise and cope in the face of adversity. It also includes being able to develop potential, work productively and creatively, build strong and positive relationships with others and contribute to the community".

For me, though, the best definition is detailed in the Chartered Institute of Personnel and Development's (CIPD) 2016 report on 'Growing The Health and Well-being Agenda' in which they set out the challenge for employers as "creating an environment to promote a state of contentment which allows an employee to flourish and achieve their full potential for the benefit of themselves and their organisation".

In a nutshell then, workplace wellbeing is about feeling good enough to flourish.
So how do we as business leaders enable our people to thrive?

Firstly, we need to understand what this entails.

Of course, to feel good about working for a company, people need to enjoy what they do, they need to feel engaged, have a strong sense of belonging, be working towards a shared purpose and feel sufficiently recognised and rewarded.

People also need to feel like they are cared about, should they encounter stress or other problems at work. They should know that solutions will be provided.

But wellbeing is about more than ensuring employee engagement and mental stability; it's about enabling staff the get the most from themselves and their job, so they can be their best selves in an environment where they feel supported.

In fact, when looking at wellbeing in any capacity, whether at work or in life, we cannot omit the field of positive psychology, which is the science of optimal human functioning.

Since its inception in 1995, positive psychology aims to discover and promote the factors that enable individuals and communities to thrive. So, whereas traditional psychology has always focused on getting people from mentally ill to neutral, positive psychology focuses on what one of the field's co-founders, Dr Christopher Peterson, calls "north of neutral", getting people from neutral to flourishing.

After decades of research, together with another founding father of Positive Psychology, Professor Martin Seligman, six core wellbeing components were established. This was partly due to the need to be able to measure wellbeing after psychologists realised that happiness, a fleeting feeling, was not as measurable as life satisfaction and that these six measurable pillars of wellbeing need to be attended to in order to optimise human functioning and life satisfaction, to enable people to flourish rather than languish.

These six 'pillars' of wellbeing form an acronym – PERMA-V:

P – Positive Emotion

E - Engagement
R - Relationships
M - Meaning
A - Achievement
V – Vitality

These apply to wellbeing in life, but we can also apply them to wellbeing at work, some more than others.

Workplace wellbeing is not just about going from overwhelmed and stressed-out to normal. I'm interested in how leaders can help make their places of work responsible for boosting wellbeing rather than merely maintaining it. Just like positive psychology focuses on optimal human functioning and taking people 'north of neutral' towards a sustainable flourishing set point of wellbeing, I believe companies should focus on taking their people north of neutral and doing all they can to enable their people to thrive.

How can we help our staff get 'north of neutral' so they are engaged, happy and therefore productive? How can we help our people to flourish and thrive at work?

Evidently, engagement is just one part of the wellbeing puzzle. At work, it is probably the most influencing factor, but it is not the only factor.

So let's explore each of the pillars of wellbeing from a workplace perspective.

Positive Emotion

"Pleasure in the job puts perfection in the work."
Aristotle

If you don't enjoy work, you're not going to put your best self into it. When you enjoy what you do at work, it gives you joy and other positive emotions, such as inspiration, gratitude and hope.

Certainly, these positive emotions are more likely to be felt when people feel content coming to work each day, so that they look forward to Monday morning rather than dread it. To make Monday mornings delightful rather than mournful, we need our workforces to love what they do so much that they are intrinsically motivated to do it and therefore do it well.

Says author of *The Happiness System for Women*, Alexandra Watson, "In this country we tend to see struggle is a badge of honour, but there's no honour in struggle. If we can give up that perception, we're a lot closer to happiness,"

And leaders need to lead the way with this. When you love what you do, it's easy to inspire others.

As Confucius said, "Choose a job you love and you will never have to work a day in your life."

"If you don't enjoy doing your job, you're not going to want to put your best self into it," adds Alexandra. "You need to ask yourself what are you trading your time in for? Because this is it. So it should be something you're in love with, something which brings out your passion and gets you fired up."

To boost positive emotions in the workplace, leaders can:

- Encourage positive talk to instil gratitude. Talk about progress made, strengths used and outcomes achieved. Ask people to jot down what they are grateful for about their job each week.
- Encourage acts of kindness in the workplace. It's been scientifically proven that kindness provides more than a good feeling for recipients, but also provides what's known as a 'givers glow' – boosting the wellbeing of the person being kind.
- Encourage people to savour the moments that they enjoy the most, to mindfully feel in their bodies a sense of gratitude for the task or the people or whatever is lighting them up.
- Encourage people to seek out inspiration in the workplace; to write down who has inspired them this week and why. This can be used to recognise those who inspire others too.

Furthermore, Barbara Fredrickson, a positivity researcher has discovered that the more positive emotions we feel over the course of our lives, the better we become at bouncing back from adversity; so the more resilient we become.

In her book, *The Little Book of Resilience*, Cheryl Rickman explains:

"Resilience is part of what psychologists call, 'psychological capital'. Fredrickson came up with the 'broaden and build' theory: when we experience positive emotions, our cognitive abilities are improved and BROADEN, making us more open to possibilities and solutions. (Conversely, negative emotions close down our capacity to think straight and cloud our judgement.)"

So the more positive emotions we feel, the more resilient we become and the better our cognitive abilities are. As such, it can be useful for employees and leaders to know their "iResilience" personality profile. For resilient people have the capacity to sustain successful performance and positive wellbeing amid adverse conditions and adjust well to change.

The iResilience report, designed by Professor Sir Cary Cooper, measures the four components of resilience according to Robertson Cooper's model. These are confidence, purposefulness, social support and adaptability. (You can get your free online resilience report here: www.robertsoncooper.com/Iresilience)

Just as wellbeing science illustrates, the ability to build strong relationships with others and have a clear sense of purpose is crucial when it comes to performing at our best. And, the more competent and confident we feel and the more flexible and adaptable we are to changing conditions equips us to better cope with the inevitable change so common in today's ever-changing business landscape.

Engagement

When it comes to workplace wellbeing, engagement is certainly one of the highest priorities, so we'll explore it in detail over the following pages.

With that in mind, it's often surprising to read how low the level of engagement is for employees and how high the percentage of this low level of engagement is, across multiple industries. Yet, keeping people fully engaged isn't an easy task. We each have different motivators, strengths and goals as individuals. However, it is possible to engage the talent we hire if we, as leaders, consider the following factors:

To maximise employee engagement:
1. Employees feel a sense of personal development and achievement.
2. The nature of work should be considered 'good work'.
3. Employees feel sufficiently motivated, recognised, appreciated and rewarded.
4. Employees find 'flow' as they love what they do and become absorbed in their tasks.
5. Employees use their signature character strengths in addition to skills and expertise.
6. The working environment is positive and engaging.

1. Personal Development and Achievement

Achievement is one of the pillars of wellbeing as set out by positive psychologists, so we'll explore that as a separate contributor as we consider each pillar.

2. Nature of Work

To feel good at work, the work needs to be deemed as 'good work'. It makes sense that the job *itself* is a prime source of motivation.

According to studies, good work should be engaging, so not monotonous or repetitive. Work should also be sufficiently secure with adequate autonomy, so people feel in control of the tasks they carry out with minimal micro-management; there should be a strong sense of 'procedural justice' and a good observance of fairness, including a fair balance between effort put in and rewards received.

Workers also need to feel they have the skills to cope under pressure, the scope to achieve their own personal goals and develop sufficiently, and good social capital in the form of supportive workplace relationships. It's no wonder that some of these criteria, such as 'relationships' and 'achievement' overlap with the core pillars of wellbeing.

Additionally, to feel engaged staff need to be aware of:
- What is expected of them?
- How their role fits into the wider organisation. i.e. how

their role makes a difference and contributes to the overall objectives and vision of the company?

- How the company is performing?

Staff who are informed about what's going on within the business, how the business is doing and where they fit into it are likely to provide a better and more focused service to customers than those who don't. As such, communication can positively or adversely affect such critical success factors as repeat custom, customer loyalty and spending-per-customer.

Secondly, while challenge is stimulating, the workload should be manageable to avoid counter-productive stress.

As well as being approachable on a daily basis, management should also meet regularly with staff to help them optimize performance. While the staff member should create a results-led action plan and outline in the meeting how they intend to implement those actions and achieve those results before the next meeting; it is up to the manager to outline how they can support those priorities, keep the role interesting and, should the actions or results be unfulfilled, coach the member of staff and/or discuss how to make the action plan more achievable. Gradually the staff member will be self-motivated to solve their own problems and meet their targets without intervention.

How to Engage via the Nature of The Work
- Ensure staff are truly engaged in the work they are doing and find it interesting.

- Provide people with the opportunities to talk to the right clients/team members so they can have a true impact on the business.
- Provide clear objectives and tools, outline expectations and set priorities. Review goals regularly and discover how you can help. Enable contribution and offer support.
- Provide the gift of awareness to your staff. Give a daily short rundown of what's going on. Don't shield them from challenges, include them in the conversation.
- Match expectations. Give people realistic expectations of what they're going to get out of a role. Ensure people are clear about what is expected of them and what the rewards will be.

3. Motivation, Recognition, Appreciation and Reward

Now that money is no longer a prime motivator, what can we do to pay into the 'emotional bank accounts' of our staff?

While the general nature of work should be deemed as 'good', people also need to feel engaged and motivated to perform at their best and to want to stick around. That means leaders need to find out precisely what makes each individual tick and motivate them accordingly.

Our shared human instinct is that we all want to feel heard and understood. As humans, intrinsically we need to have that.

From the moment we interview people to join our workforces, it's vital to listen to them and show an interest in their whole selves, not just to know where to put them within the organisation to thrive but also to unearth what makes them tick? That's when everyone wins.

Uncover: What inspires them to take action? How the role fits with their own personal development agenda? Who are they outside of work? What are their interests? And what does their ideal day look like? Find out what fascinates and excites them?

Uncover what motivating factors each member of staff will best respond to?

Is it peer recognition? Is it level of responsibility? Or perhaps the provision of opportunities to grow?

For Teresa Boughey, author of *Closing the Gap: 5 Steps to Creating an Inclusive Culture*, only when we enable employees to know themselves and celebrate themselves can we, as leaders, begin to know, celebrate, recognise and reward their capabilities.

Fiona McDonnell concurs. "Engagement is about saying, 'How do we value and celebrate the things that people do? And how do organisations create programmes to really recognise the contributions not just on the business metrics?," says Fiona, who recommends establishing different types of employee recognition schemes as a way to recognise and reward talent on a number of fronts.

Cheerleading is such an important part of the engagement process. By encouraging our people to encourage each other, through nominating their own workforce for great things they've done, we can shine a spotlight on people's key strengths, on what we recognise they do really well.

How to Engage via Recognition, Appreciation and Reward

- Recognise achievements by praising, rewarding and promoting your team based on performance. Tell people when they have done a good job. Stage regular employee appreciation events to congratulate and thank top performers, motivate staff and share your vision.
- Set up an employee recognition scheme and invite nominations from team members to recognise what other members of the team have done well. Ensure that everyone gets recognised, so nobody feels left out.
- Incentivise staff with a range of performance-related incentives. From flight tokens and discount cards to group away days to Royal Ascot.
- Consider non-cash alternatives to cash bonuses, such as extra days holiday, shopping vouchers, retailer discount cards or air miles.
- Provide staff with the opportunity to share in the success of the business via shares and share options. This gives talent a vested interest in adding value to

enhance the performance of the company and gives them good reason to stick around to realise the value of their shareholding.

- Ensure that you have clear measures of performance so that you will know when bonuses or incentives have been earned. Performance related rewards can be only be effective where they can be measurable.
- Align rewards with company goals and customer feedback. Let customers tell you who are the best performers in their eyes. Such feedback can improve customer referral rates and satisfaction rates simultaneously.

4. Finding Their Forte

Using our skills and expertise makes us feel good. As Leendert Den Hollander says about the type of work which is the most engaging for people, "If you can bring together what you enjoy and what you're good at, then you'll have something magic".

Signature Strengths
However, there's another way to optimise our enjoyment of our work - by deploying our signature character strengths whilst we perform our tasks. These energize and engage us and also lead to peak performance.

Signature strengths are different to skills and expertise.

Founding fathers of the positive psychology movement, Christopher Peterson and Martin Seligman, defined 24 signature character strengths which we all have to varying degrees.

The most accurate way to determine our own signature strengths is to take the scientifically validated "VIA (Values in Action) Inventory of Strengths" survey, a free (and incredibly accurate) online test featuring 120 questions at www.viacharacter.org. The survey ranks individual strengths in order.

Once you and your people know their top five strengths, it's important to do work which deploys those signature strengths. This has been proven to boost wellbeing. In a controlled diary study, usage of character strengths repaired bad mood and positively affected mood the following day. Furthermore, a study carried out in 2005 by Professor Seligman showed that those who deployed their signature strengths in a novel way each day for a week increased happiness and decreased depression and stress for between three and six months, results which a Human Resource Management study of 442 employees across 39 departments in eight organisations corroborated, also proving that "strengths-based psychological climate was linked with improved work performance".

Developing Self-Awareness
Of course, you can only know what you love and what your strengths are when you know yourself, when you have a

sufficient level of self-awareness that you understand who you are and what you bring to the world. As such, it's worthwhile providing staff with ways to get to know and understand themselves better.

As well as the VIA survey, you might point them towards Myers Briggs personality testing which, again very accurately, identifies which of 16 different personality types you are most aligned to, and, crucially, the way you take on information, make decisions, and deal with the outer world.

These in-depth surveys can paint a clear picture of who each individual is and where their strengths lie and can therefore work well in addition to simply chatting to uncover what excites them, what they love to do and what they feel most skilled at?

Knowing our strengths helps us perform to the best of our ability and be more likely to achieve our purpose goals too.

As Alexandra Watson, author of *The Happiness System For Women*, says, "The oldest teaching on the planet from various places throughout time and history has been 'Know yourself'. Know who you really are, not who you might think you are", says Alexandra, who tells the women she coaches that they are often so much more than they think they are.

She goes on to say, "Once you have true authentic confidence in who you are and what you're doing - then everybody else tends to play along with that. I always liken it to - you teach people how to treat you."

I've certainly found that to be true, the more self-aware and self-confident I've become as I've grown to know myself better, the better I've been treated by others.

In this way self-knowledge earns respect, something worth remembering as business leaders. The more we know ourselves, the better people can know who we are. We get better at showing up as our true selves. This is helpful to those we lead as it has a contagious effect of inspiring others to do the same.

Back when I was struggling to understand where I belonged in the world, I was unsure about who I was and what my strengths and weaknesses were. These days, I know I'm creative, engaging and I thoroughly enjoy speaking with people and meeting new people every day. Talking with people about topics of interest causes me to lose track of time and find a state of flow and I gain feedback from people through what they say back to me.

This sense of flow is integral to feeling engaged.

Fiona McDonnell concurs, "When you understand what you're good at and what you're passionate about – which aren't necessarily the same thing – and if you can do work which combines those two things, that's when you can get in the zone."

"Combining that with the humility to learn and adapt along the way is important," adds Fiona, who's own personal journey has seen her become a more versatile and collaborative leader while ensuring she has still remained focused on her strengths.

Enabling your staff to get into that zone of optimal engagement is a huge wellbeing booster.

5. Finding Their Flow

Once people know what they're most talented in and what their signature character strengths are, they cannot only excel, they can ramp their level of engagement up a notch.

Engaging work is the kind we can truly immerse ourselves in. When we do this, we can find 'flow' otherwise known as 'optimal experience', a state of sustained involvement and heightened engagement coined by Hungarian psychologist Mihaly Csikszentmihalyi, to describe what happens when we participate in activities which absorb and engage us so much that we lose track of time or feel like nothing else matters.

Flow is the feeling athletes get when they forget the crowd is there or the feeling musicians have when they feel 'one with the music'.

During flow we can park everyday stressors and achieve peak performance. However, this state isn't our status quo, as we ordinarily tend to question ourselves during our activities rather than allow ourselves to get fully engrossed in them. But, when we do, it's incredibly satisfying, engaging and, as such, a booster of our wellbeing. Research has also found that flow states improve our creativity levels.

This state of wellbeing optimises our experience and engagement, thus improving the quality of our experience at work.

So how do we and the talent we hire find this state of optimal experience?

- Consider tasks which balance capability and challenge. These activities generally need to be not too easy and not too difficult, so challenging enough, but not so difficult that we lose enjoyment.
- Enable feedback about how you are doing while you are doing it. According to research by Mihaly Csikszentmihalyi, flow-inducing activities should be "achievable, controllable and focused, with the potential to receive feedback during participation." So there needs to be an ability to gauge how well we are doing as we focus our attention on the task at hand.

Of course, just as what we do is important when it comes to workplace engagement, so too is *where* we do it.

6. Positive Working Environment

An encouraging and energising environment is so key to engagement and workplace wellbeing. A pleasing space in which to work will have up-to-date equipment, ergonomically designed working areas, natural light, access to drinking water, hot drinks and plenty of plants to allow a good flow of oxygen and cultivate calm.

Outdoor eating and meeting areas are also worth investing in to enable people to grab some fresh air and a good dose of natural light to recharge.

The general vibe and atmosphere should also help people feel happy, included and valued.

A playful and colourful space will have a far more positive impact on creativity and productivity than a dull grey one will.

From the colour of the walls to the layout of the working environment, from little touches such as including praise for employees on the walls or ceiling or, as Red Bull have done in London, installing a slide to take people from one floor to the next; from making Friday a 'free cake for employees' day, to putting fresh flowers, sofas or beanbags in meeting rooms; from celebrating successes and rewarding the team with a spa treatment or ordering in pizza for lunch, there is much to be said for creating a pleasant, fun and motivational environment where 'wins' are celebrated in a pleasant working space. Doing so can generate a spark which jumpstarts the creative process while such levity also has the power to boost morale and trust, enabling people to perform better and achieve more.

While positive and fun surroundings and activities boost productivity, creativity, and loyalty, having a fun-loving manager at the helm also encourages staff retention.

According to a survey by Ipsos, staff with managers with an "above average" sense of humour are 90% likely remain in their jobs compared to 77.5% with non-fun managers.

Similarly, The Great Place to Work Institute has revealed that providing a "fun environment" classifies 81% of companies as 'great' rather than merely 'good'. And people don't want to leave places of work that are great; where camaraderie is nurtured and people feel a part of something, as we've explored in the Chapter on Purpose.

"You can easily recognise a productive workplace – it's the one where the people look as though they're having a good time,"
Brian Chernett, Founder of The Academy for Chief Executives

Relationships

Camaraderie can only be felt among positive relationships and one of the core pillars of wellbeing is supportive relationships.

It's well reported that good company is good for us; that strong supportive connections are a vital component of our wellbeing and help mitigate stress.

Connection with others is also mission-critical commercially, so the value of a good solid supportive network is high. And, as AI and digital technology usage rises, emotional intelligence will become an even more valuable commodity. As people seek to differentiate their skills and traditional roles within the workforce change – what will allow our differentiation will be our ability to communicate and develop deep and personal connected relationships.

This is why it's important as business leaders to have our own inner hut (our 'virtual boardroom' if you will) and to enable the people we work with to cultivate their own supportive connections within our companies.

A lot of business leaders will tell you the importance of surrounding yourself with the right people as they've learned the hard way by hiring a lot of the wrong people. I would be one of them.

That's why it's important for you to cultivate a good relationship with yourself, so you know:

- The kind of people who light you up and the kinds of people who bring you down
- The kind of people who have the ability to do what you can't; those who fill the gaps in your own skillset, mindset and character strengths

For me, in the early days, I thought I could do everything myself. I learnt very quickly that I couldn't. You can't be in control of everything and do everything well. It just doesn't add up. So, as a leader, you need to genuinely empower people to make decisions for you, and you need to allow them to make their own mistakes, as hard as that is, because that's the best way that they are going to learn.

As well as surrounding yourself with the right people, people who have your back – an inner hut of people who you can always rely on – you also need a virtual boardroom; people who inspire and motivate you.

For example, in my own virtual boardroom, my husband Costa Peter Delis is my pillar of strength. He understands my personal drive. Being a business leader himself, he's great to run my ideas past.

Jinlong Wang, The CEO and Chairman of PizzaExpress is another inhabitant in my virtual boardroom. He's an unassuming but quietly confident business leader who I've had the good fortune to gather wisdom from each time I've stumbled into his office. His polite, humble and courteous nature is inspiring, as is his passion for making a difference and, as a Chinese business leader with significant Western cultural experiences I feel a strong sense of kinship with him.

The same is true of Ton Christiaanse, a straight-talking Dutch man, with whom I did a fireside podcast chat recently. He is a very kind-hearted man and I always enjoy our chats! As the CEO of Aviko group, he believes in servant leadership and that the classical hierarchy should be turned upside down. I love how he describes the classic hierarchical matrix as an "upside down Christmas tree"! Ton advocates for young people in the board room, not just as token youngsters in an advisory capacity but as knowledgeable and digitised folk who understand today's world. That perspective, along with mindsets from diverse backgrounds, nationalities, genders and ages, is critical in creating boardroom balance.

Another virtual boardroom member of mine is Sam Allen of Sam Allen Associates Executive Search. Sam is one of my 'sheroes' and has been a wonderful mentor to me. She's in my virtual boardroom as I aspire to have her personal touch. She makes me and those she works with feel like they really matter, which makes her an invaluable member and she has guided me towards success.

Another member is super successful Brian Kennedy, Chairman of Latium Enterprises, for his vision and belief and ability to launch businesses from simplistic ideas to often complex reality. His resilience and tenacity as well as his ability to bounce back from failure is something I learnt early on when I embarked on my entrepreneurial journey. I often remind myself of the importance of these traits at times of hardship or when launching or embarking upon a new business venture.

Leann Hearne, Group CEO of First Ark Group, is another wonderful woman and friend in my virtual boardroom. I personally love spending time with Leanne, as she's so down to earth and gives great advice for aspiring leaders, especially those passionate about embracing their best and most authentic self in both business and personally.

Mark Metry is another of my virtual inhabitants. Mark battled with various health and mental disorders at a young age and went on to launch the world's most successful Minecraft server at the age of 15! His realisation as a result of his journey in life is that the best way to live your life is to forge your own path and identity.

Ian John Toal, Chief executive officer, Alfaco is another dear friend of mine and frequent visitor to my virtual boardroom. Ian has gravitas and presence like no other that I have met in the world of business. His words and advice have and always will pack and punch across any boardroom. He has this intrinsic ability to be able to read though a situation that I may find complex and make it very simple. Many a time has Ian read though a situation I have discussed with him and without even blinking given me a very simple solution. Not always one I have wanted to hear but one which is exactly what I have needed to hear and action!

Campbell Fitch is a forthright Scotsman and Chief People Office who speaks with sincerity and from the heart. Campbell is both a mentor and a sponsor to me as he is willing to truly champion people and causes he believes in. He has this innate ability to read people, situations and scenarios down to the tee. Campbell's stories are effusively told and he never fails to leave you with a golden nugget of wisdom to take away. Everyone should have a Campbell in their virtual boardroom!

Of course, my hardworking mother, my hero of a father, and my wise owl of a brother Michael are also regulars in my virtual boardroom – each person brings with them a different quality to the boardroom table.

In my virtual boardroom I also have people I've not met but who can impart their wisdom and help me to grow and move forward with my ideas – people who inspire, encourage and teach me.

Like Paul Polman, former CEO of Unilever, Co-founder/Chair of IMAGINE and Vice-Chair of the U.N. Global Compact. Paul founded the Kilimanjaro Blind Trust and supports and mentors young leaders as a Counsellor and Chair of the Global Advisory Board of One Young World.

And Leena Nair, the first female Chief HR Officer of Unilever. He global people agenda spans across 160,000 employees in over 100 countries. Says Lena, "My agenda ensures we have the right people in the right roles, with the right capabilities and mindset to decouple growth from its environmental footprint whilst increasing its positive social impact."

She's a woman after my own heart as her own personal goal is "to build an inclusive environment where all members of our diverse society can contribute and succeed in equal measure."

192

Consider who is in your own virtual boardroom and why? List them below. What qualities do they have that you aspire to and how do they support you?

My Virtual Boardroom:

_____
_____
_____
_____
_____
_____

Also consider what can you give back to them?

I gain a lot from every person in my 'inner hut' – that cherished virtual boardroom. But relationships are about give and take, so it's important to give as much as we take from that support. Giving before receiving makes the world a better place.

Deepening Your Connections By Giving

The value of a network is imperative to business success. My recommendations for growing a network are personal touches and genuine interest in someone for who they are and what they do.

In a world that is social media focused, mass mailer centric and surface level only it is vital to foster connections on a more deep and meaningful level. Personal non-generic messages are therefore key.

I've spent many a weekend writing personal notes or messages to leaders and even going as far as to personally deliver Christmas cards to their Head Offices and handwrote letters to every single one of the FTSE 350 directors to whom I gifted a book. Some of them responded and one told me he had the book in his office and often read quotes to his staff from it!

Personal touches make you memorable.

Giving time and effort at one end of the funnel of a relationship reaps rewards later on. It's all about planting seeds in a garden to create a strong and supportive network. The more seeds you plant, the more your garden will have an opportunity to grow. You then have to nurture and nourish those seedlings of your relationships.

That's how I've secured meetings with top people from some of the top companies like Amazon, Sainsbury's and Marks and Spencer. One remembered me as the person who'd sent him the book in the post.

Supportive relationships help you feel like you're safe, provide you with the level of encouragement and support that boosts your sense of wellbeing but also, from a commercial perspective, provides opportunity after opportunity. After all, one of the greatest compliments in business is a positive referral.

So, to nurture supportive relationships in leadership:
- Try to remember one personal fact and one business fact about each person you meet. For example, 'how is your wife Jane and your children? Isn't one of them about to start secondary school now?'
- Researching people's background before meeting with them is a must if you want to cultivate strong long-term relationships.
- Consider personal touches so you make people feel important. Always seek out ways you can go the extra mile and give a little more.
- Have a virtual boardroom of people you can rely on to support/encourage you and be in other people's virtual boardroom as a supporter and encourager.

Meaning

That our work is meaningful is a key contributor to our wellbeing. We want to feel like we're contributing to a wider shared purpose and vision; that we're part of something.

Purpose gives our lives meaning. Doing purposeful work is critical to our wellbeing in the workplace. Service and contribution generate a sense of purpose which gives our lives meaning and also generates what Aristotle called 'eudaemonic happiness', which derives from the Greek words *eu*("good") and *daimõn* ("spirit").

Feeling like we are a part of something gives our lives meaning, a sense of belonging and a reassuring feeling of trust and identity.

We can help those who work for and with us to find meaning in their work by giving them a sense of purpose. Refer back to Chapter 5 where we explore Purposeful Leadership in-depth for more detailed ideas on how to do just that.

Something that all leaders can do to bring more meaning to people's roles is to help their workforce to be able to clearly articulate their own personal vision for what they'd like to accomplish, as this is what spurs us on to work purposefully and provide meaning. This also helps people to formulate goals that will help them achieve that vision of personal success; those intentional actions become a yardstick for measuring personal growth. Hence why 'meaning' and 'achievement' are two core pillars of wellbeing which are intrinsically linked.

Achievement

In many ways people are like plants. To cultivate their potential and help them flourish and grow we need to water the shoots of their ideas, encourage their growth with the right support and provide the right environment to enable them to reach their potential. As such, talent needs to be cultivated.

Both ideas and personal development goals should be nourished.

Nourish Ideas

Ideas fuel growth; particularly in an economy that is changing at an exponential pace. So it's important to give employees a sense of ownership over decision-making processes and the ultimate vision and provide a culture which stimulates innovation and provides a platform for individual and team creativity.

Conversely, companies which fail to encourage and nurture ideas will lose the people having those ideas along with the ideas themselves. Those people will simply leave and set up on their own or join a competitor who not only listens to their ideas, but puts them into action. None of us want the best ideas to walk out of the door with our best people.

Personal Development

People who can identify a long-term opportunity in joining your business are more likely to stay. Commit to designing a long-term career structure for people and they will commit to *your* business over the long-term.

And, given that accomplishment is one of the core pillars of wellbeing, by helping your people on their journey to achieve their goals, you are simultaneously bolstering their level of wellbeing.

Unless you listen to people and understand people's motivations and desires, you can't help them achieve their ambitions.

Yes, they may well be motivated by the commission and bonuses and share-option schemes; gym membership, dental cover and health insurance may be nice. But, to *really* understand what motivates them, you need to understand where they want to go! What do they want to achieve?

As we discovered previously, personal growth and room to achieve their own goals in a key contributor to how engaged and motivated a person feels at work. With that in mind, it's important that leaders uncover people's self-actualisation drivers. Where do they see themselves in five years' time and how can you help them realise their career aspirations within your company? Provide people with personal growth opportunities:

- Help people to develop their talent and key strengths rather than focusing on their weaknesses. Invest in staff training and development, mentoring and coaching, vocational learning, volunteering opportunities.
- Hold regular one to one meetings not only to discuss plans of action and the future needs of the business, but also to discuss your staff member's own performance, their career journey and developmental needs. Enable staff to self-appraise where possible.
- Foster a work culture that offers strong a collaborative and communicative management style, and an organisational culture in which learning and development are encouraged.

When people feel they are headed in the right direction and that they'll achieve their personal development goals in their journey within your company, they'll feel good and be more likely to stay on that journey with you.

There's one more vital wellbeing pillar to consider. This was only added to the list of factors that people need to optimally function when it was realised that you could tick all the PERMA boxes but, without decent sleep, exercise and general energy-boosting factors, a lack of self-care could be detrimental to the rest of the factors.

Vitality

When the concept of wellbeing at work first seized the headlines, the assumption was that this meant provision of incentives to help workforces stay physically healthy. However, wellbeing is as much about mental, psychological and emotional health as physical health. Indeed, as we've learned, wellbeing needs to be tackled from a whole person and organisation perspective.

With this in mind, while health and vitality are an important part of the conversation, but so too is the work itself; *i.e.* it's no good dishing out free fruit and subsidized gym membership if you're not also addressing workload, equal pay, flexible working hours, autonomy, engagement, recognition and belonging, among other key factors covered in this chapter.

That said, physical health can have a significant impact on psychological health, so good leaders need to proactively support both.

- Establish walking meetings – walking is good for physical and mental health, especially if in a natural setting. According to a Stanford University study, walking makes us between 60 and 80 per cent more creative, compared to sitting still, with this creative boost effect lasting long after we've sat down again. Steve Jobs, Ludvig van Beethoven, Charles Darwin and Charles Dickens each walked for miles every day.

- Set up outdoor meeting areas. Being outdoors is better for us than being indoors.
  Even better, if you can include eco-therapy activities, such as mini vegetable gardens or outdoor gym activities or even provision of natural environments such as a bio-diversity garden through which to walk, you can foster mental wellness as these engage the parasympathetic nervous system and help lower stress and anxiety. There is so much research to support being in nature as a natural antidepressant too.

- Encourage regular outdoor breaks. This is for two reasons. 1). Nature enables what psychologists call "attention restoration", giving our over-stimulated brains the opportunity to rest and recover. 2). As well as boosting our energy levels and mood, walking in nature helps us to think more clearly and sparks creativity too.

- Assess switch-off time outside of work too and reward self-care. In France, employees have 'the right to disconnect'. It's important for employees, entrepreneurs and leaders to give their brains a break and recharge. As such, it's up to us as business leaders to ensure we and our people are not scrolling through work emails late at night. Incentivising self-care can be a good way to ensure people are taking care of themselves and this goes for you, Dear Reader, too.

- Provide mental health and wellbeing training. For example, staff can be trained how to manage common mental health conditions, such as depression and anxiety, and can get training in stress management, resilience, mindfulness, cognitive behavioural therapy (CBT), time management and financial wellbeing.

- Invest time in exploring initiatives that can help you improve your workplace's wellbeing and knowledge of managing mental health. Initiatives such as Britain's Healthiest Workplace free online survey for employers and employees is available to all employers with 20 or more employees. See www.vitality.co.uk/business/healthiest-workplace

Other initiatives include: Minds@Work which aims to inspire and empower individuals to break the stigma of mental ill health in their organisations. Founder Geoff McDonald, ex-Global VP of HR at Unilever, wants to create a world where everybody in every workplace feels they genuinely have the choice to put up their hand and ask for help when they are suffering from

mental   ill   health.   See
www.mindsatworkmovement.com

Mental health communication firm, Mates in Mind, is another charitable initiative which enables people to talk openly with their employer and colleagues or 'mental health first-aiders' about mental health issues.

- Proactively enable work-life balance. Offer flexible working hours, including shift switching and the freedom to work from home, as it can have an even greater impact than feeling supported and cared for. For example, by using the time they'd have spent commuting to work to get more sleep, exercise or connect with family members, your people can boost their wellbeing and be more productive as a result. The ability to work from home and use tools such as Zoom or Skype for meetings can give people the freedom to take their children to school, walk the dog through the woods, make a hearty breakfast and switch their computer on and still start work at the same time they would've done had they been working at the office. Also consider offering extra holiday as an incentive for completing projects to deadline. As long as staff hit their KPIs and achieve their targets, they should have flexibility about how they balance this workload with maintaining their wellbeing.

Virgin Media Group went one step further and, following Netflix's lead, introduced unlimited annual leave to its workers in 2014. This means Virgin Media staff can take time off whenever they wish on the proviso that they take responsibility for still fulfilling their duties and on the understanding they only take leave when they are certain they and their team are up to speed on projects and that their absence won't be detrimental. As long as employers abide by the law of allowing a minimum of 28 days paid annual leave (in the UK, that is), this initiative can work well to give workers autonomy.

Another company which has proven to take the whole wellbeing of their staff seriously is travel fare aggregator, Skyscanner, for whom 95% of their 800 employees across 10 offices around the world report feeling that the company ensures their wellbeing at work. The 'Healthiest New Entrant' in the Britain's Healthiest Workplace awards won recognition for their wellbeing initiatives encompassing good working practices, leisure and physical and mental health. For example, as well as a share incentive plan and company bonus scheme, the company offers extra annual leave available to buy, subsidized massages, free fruit juices and barista coffee machines, along with leisure activities from foosball and table tennis to Xbox and Playstation game consoles.

Fundamentally though, wellbeing in the workplace is more than what you provide via opportunities to get outdoors or play or find flow – it is about how you make people feel good and how you enable people to grow within a safe and supportive place.

Just as Claude Silver, Chief Heart Officer at VaynerMedia, says of her role where to gets to speak to people internally and externally about "the need to treat employees like humans and not numbers; I have the honour of watching 800 people grow!"

And that honour of witnessing humanity and enabling growth, in both a human and commercial sense, is what being a leader in 2020 and beyond is all about.

Chapter 7 - The Millennial Way

"Alone we can do so little; together we can do so much,"
Helen Keller

The New Workforce

Experts forecast that Millennials (those born between 1981 and 1996) will make up 75% of the entire workforce by 2025, changing the composition of our modern workplace and leadership forever.

With many already in their late 30s, the Millennial Generation have, according to Pew Research Centre, already surpassed Generation Xers as the largest workforce demographic in the US (35% of all workers).

And so, over the next decade, Millennials will gradually globally occupy more and more leadership roles and take over critical decision-making responsibility for people's working lives.

The impact is noteworthy because, unlike our predecessors, Millennials frankly won't stay in a job where we feel undervalued or marginalised. Although the stereotype of the entitled and lazy job-hopper is an exaggeration, it is true that, on average, Millennials change jobs every two years. Due in part to a lack of engagement, purpose and opportunity at work, but also due to the Millennial motivation of constant growth, purpose and meaning.

Yes, Millennials are mobile and flexible and want to do work which is meaningful. And, given the way they've grown up with constant connection to information (both true and false), Millennials have learned to be curious about what they are told and, as such are a particularly questioning and listening generation.

A Different World View and Work View

And it's no wonder, the Millennial generation has grown up in a world where corporations and their leaders have been reported to be up to no good; where fake news has proliferated and led to an array of political and corporate storms, and in an economy which saw their parents and older peers enduring a recession and, in many cases, losing their jobs as a result.

These circumstances have created a generation of people who are self-starters; keen to build and create; a generation with little trust in traditional hierarchal leadership and one which questions and examines to find the truth, rather than blindly accept it; a gift for organisations which value innovation.

As a direct consequence of the circumstances in which Generation Y has grown up, transparency is within the comfort zone of Millennials who have grown up in a world richly diverse in gender, race and sexual orientation and, as such, more liberal and open.

What's more, digital natives have been raised with instant (and constant) access to the internet, so are more connected, aware of and therefore open to a varied range of perspectives, choices, lifestyles and ideas.

This openness frees Millennials from the constraints that previous generations have been confronted with. Millennials are perfectly comfortable having those uncomfortable conversations and are open to hearing from everyone, given the equal importance placed on everyone's voices, which Millennials seek out and listen to.

Remember, Millennials grew up within a world of social networking, a world where each and every individual is unique and special.

As such, Millennials have a truly egalitarian perspective where titles matter less than equal opportunities. It's not the title of leadership which attracts 95% of those surveyed by Deloitte who were keen to lead but the action of leading. What's important to note, is the kind of leadership which Millennials value and aspire to, driven by how they've come through life. For Millennials value and aspire towards people-centric leadership, where empathy and self-respect significantly outrank hierarchy and power.

Fundamentally, Millennials want to lead and it's important for existing leaders to empower them to do so at the earliest opportunity, rather than wait until no longer having a choice.

Why? Because Millennials can capitalise on how they are wired; they can harness their connectivity, they can tap into their empathy and they can use their openness to lead diverse and inclusive teams where everyone feels like they belong.

In doing so, Millennials will create a workplace where those with varying perspectives all get to participate and innovate; teams where individuals feel seen, heard, empowered, engaged and purposeful –teams filled with people who want to continue to work for their company as the grow, rather than just go (to another company).

Millennials understand and encourage diversity because they're living it. The Millennial workforce is far more diverse than older generations.

As a Millennial myself, I know that our unique way of seeing the world has a lot to do with us being the most diverse generation (culturally, racially and sexually) to have ever worked. This is why we don't just see diversity as it has traditionally been seen, *i.e.* as a race, equality, demographics and representation issue; rather, Millennials see workforce diversity as more cognitive, *i.e.* as the collaboration, validation and fusion of a wide variety of different backgrounds, experiences, viewpoints and perspectives.

Today, companies need this different Millennial world view for a different working world. The workplace landscape is constantly changing, so those leading these perpetually shifting working environments must harness the power of the generation which is used to change, which knows how to navigate it and, in doing so, ride the waves of change toward a more inclusive and innovative setting.

Sea Change

As Jennifer Brown told me during our podcast conversation, latterly, until now, a handful of individuals have been working incredibly hard to persuade leaders, person-by-person, to change. She says, "Trying to pull older organisations and older generations into this conversation has faced resistance and needed to be done person-by person, a bit like walking along the beach painstakingly tossing each starfish back into the water so they might have a chance to thrive. But I do see that changing as organisations are feeling the heat of demographic changes – both in their employee base and also in their customer base, which is becoming way more diverse."

The reasons to cultivate a more diverse and inclusive workplace go far beyond the black dollar, the female dollar, the Asian dollar or the gay dollar, of course. But, as Jennifer suggests, the writing is now on the wall. Partly because those groups are the fastest growing in terms of consumers, but also because Millennials are entering the leadership space and making a difference in this different world.

And the world of work is responding. Layers of management are shrinking as organisations flatten their hierarchies in response to these emerging and fresh perspectives. Climbing the corporate pyramid is no longer the core goal, as opportunities to lead open across multiple levels.

This generation is moving away from titles to what's *behind* the title – the *purpose* of the role and how it makes them *feel*; rather than a role's name, a role's meaning has seized priority; rather than direct reports, a network of relationships have taken centre stage. Subsequently, Millennials won't blindly follow leaders based on mere title alone.

And yet, it's a tough climate which Millennials have inherited. As global citizens, Millennials value collaboration and shared purpose amid expanded globalization. Equality is highlighted in a diverse world during a time when nations are sorely lacking in cultural alignment.

It is therefore a different challenge to the challenges faced by our predecessors and one which requires a different perspective.

Thankfully that's what Millennials have: egalitarian rather than patriarchal, global rather than national and creative rather than prescriptive.

The consequence of having different values is that Millennials see leadership differently and want to lead differently. Millennials have different priorities and needs, both as employers and employees. So, if organisations can develop Millennial leadership skills in a way which taps into this openness, flexibility and empathy, companies and their bold new workforce can thrive together.

Promising Yet Powerless

You'd think that, given all that Millennials have going for them, those running companies in today's status quo might do more to embrace the Millennial ideal of leadership and engage this generation. Sadly, statistics suggest otherwise.

According to Stanford University, compared with the late 1990s, labour market participation among teens and young adults has steeply declined from 46 percent between 1998 and 1999 to 33 percent between 2011 and 2013. Meanwhile, according to research by Deloitte, 66% of Millennials are disengaged at work. 91% of Millennials plan to leave their jobs before three years. And, when Millennials vote with their feet and leave, it costs an average of $25k.

This 'Millennial Wheel of Disengagement' appears to be partly due to a Catch 22 situation where organisations are reluctant to invest in a generation of people who may not stay with the company for long, which exacerbates the problem as Millennials are less likely to stick around when they don't see a future with their employer.

The only way to break this cycle is to invest in Millennial Leadership Development anyway, so that Millennials *do* see a future with your company.

Furthermore, to counter this Millennial Wheel of Disengagement, existing leaders need to get under the hood of the motivation of this generation; to fully understand what matters most to this new workforce?

Only then can today's organisations become Millennial-ready and help this generation of top talent to lead businesses in an altogether different way – but a way which serves the constantly changing business landscape we find ourselves in.

What Millennials Want - Embracing the Millennial Ideal of Leadership

What matters to Millennials isn't so much the creativity and fun that Baby Boomers have coveted. No, for Millennials, it's all about opportunity, possibility, flexibility, purpose and growth.

So let's explore each of these.

Opportunity and Possibility

Millennials want opportunities to build, to innovate, and to create, and that's good for business.

They also want opportunities to grow and that means the possibility of leadership needs to be open to them; the provision of leadership development specifically designed for Millennials is mission-critical. Yet, according to the Deloitte survey, 60% of Millennials had only received around one day of leadership development per year.

This illustrates a major gap in giving Millennials what they want (and what organisations need, whether or not they realise it).

Yes, Millennials need to be given the opportunity to lead. Because, when they do, the possibilities are endless. After all, many Millennials already see themselves as leading the way, whether their job title says so or not.

Millennials see themselves as leaders even though only 48 per cent of them hold official 'leadership' titles. According to leadership development firm, Virtuali, 72 per cent of Millennials consider themselves to be leaders in the workplace. What's more, Millennials are more engaged and productive when they feel a sense of ownership for their role and when they are empowered to lead and to drive their own results.

Evidently actions speak louder than words. Remember, it's not about the title; it's about feeling empowered to lead, at all levels. It's the action of leading that's important, rather than the title.

The Millennials surveyed by Deloitte in their recent Global Millennial Survey, said they want to lead and they want to lead their way. What's more, they want to make a difference. They want what they at work to have a positive impact on the world. So let's tap into this generation's enthusiasm to lead. And empower them to do so; to have the positive impact they crave by providing Millennials with sufficient leadership development and support to help them grow into the leaders they are so keen on becoming.

Growth

The opportunity to learn and grow was recently ranked at the top of a recent Gallup poll, asking Millennials what was most important to them when applying for a new job. This suggests that the best young talent will go where the growth is.

Previous generations have been keen to grow their careers but have tended to think more long term and been satisfied to grow at a slower pace. But Millennials don't just want a long-term growth plan, they want speed too. Yes, pace of progression is an important consideration too, because Millennials want short-term fast growth in their careers.

They want to tap their potential immediately, so they are looking for dynamic project or assignment-based career models which allow them to develop on the job and experience a faster pace of career growth.

Importantly, this does NOT mean they want defined succession and career plans. Millennials want mobility and flexibility so they may move around, rather than a five-year plan with only vertical movement. Because Millennials cherish a wide variety of experience; that's how they learn and grow.

Consequently, this generation prefers project-based roles rather than a clearly defined set role. That way Millennials can grow in a dynamic way where they assume responsibilities for a year or so, then shift to assume some different responsibilities, all the while learning and growing.

The direction of growth is an important consideration too. Rather than climb the ladder, they want to 'work the lattice'. Rather than climbing the career ladder over a long period of time, Millennials favour growing across a career lattice. They may grow their careers in stature, but they do so by gaining a wider wealth of experience than their predecessors, and this includes relishing the opportunity to work abroad.

According to Gartner, international work experience opportunities would make Millennials 77% more likely to remain with a company, 80% more likely to join a company and 82% more engaged at work. Working abroad would also make 90% of those surveyed more effective leaders. So global growth is a consistently highly rated career aspiration for Millennials, who've grown up in a globally connected society.

This means, to enable the Millennial generation to grow professionally, employers need to:

- Establish the right mixture of short-term individual assignments and team projects to satisfy the Generation Y hunger for change amid growth.
- Invest is sufficient training and development.
- Understand the kind of learning which Millennials favour.
- Offer exposure to global opportunities too.

Balance is therefore key as it's important for all staff to gain experience from time in a role, but Millennials need to feel engaged in order to gain that experience, so project-based assignments which enable them to sharpen their skills is key.

Says Deloitte Australia. "Why don't we run our companies more like consulting firms, where we let high potentials take 3-6 month assignments in the company as part of their career? This type of change will alter our talent management process, but it creates the dynamic type of organisation we need today."

EXERCISE: Visualisation

Invite your Millennial team members to participate in the following Visualisation Exercise.

Picture yourself having already achieved your work goals. Imagine yourself sharing your success story with others. Perhaps you're being interviewed for a magazine article or sharing your journey with friends. See everything vividly in your mind's eye – who are you talking to? What are you wearing? Where are you sharing your success story? What can you hear? What can you smell? Feel the joy and excitement of having accomplished what you set out to and vividly explore how it all came to pass – which projects did you embark on and how did each one set you in good stead to lead into the next? What experiences do you cherish the most and which people sponsored and mentored you on your journey? What did you learn from them? See your accolades on your desk, your book on the shelf and your map of the world on the wall with pins showing all the countries you've visited and worked in; visualise all that you hope to achieve as having come true.

Once your visualisation is complete, plot a route map of 5-10 tasks that would help you bring that dream to fruition and then take small steps towards making it a reality.

Change and Flexibility

Millennials have different expectations to previous generations. They don't expect a lifelong career with the same company or even in the same industry. And, while they still value the notion of a career, they've not grown up in a world of jobs for life. As a consequence, Millennials take more risks over staying safe, prioritise experiencing new things rather than gaining experience in one thing and favour the possibility of working on multiple exciting projects across the lifetime of their career.

This has caused Millennials to cherish the dynamic of constant change and thrive on innovation. Indeed, Millennials have a tendency to push for change. When people say, 'but this is the way it's always been done,' Millennials refuse to take that for an answer, instead demonstrating a new way; a Millennial way of *being* the change.

As Greta Thunberg said at the UN Climate Conference:

> *"We have not come here to beg world leaders to care.*
> *We have come to let them know change is coming."*

So, as torchbearers of change, signalling a need to shift, Millennials are expecting companies to change too – Millennials are inviting us to change an array of things, from how we appraise and reward people, and how we motivate and move people, to how we think about career progression and leadership development and, notably, how much we value purpose, collaboration, diversity and inclusion.

Whereas previous generations needed job security and the stability that came with that, Generation Y is less risk-averse; hence why large corporations are becoming more dynamic. And they need to be in order to compete for top talent.

What's more, knowing that Millennials want to make a positive impact on the world and be the change they see in it, companies need to ensure they have a clarity of purpose in order to attract and retain this purposeful generation.

Purpose

We already know how important purpose has on workers' wellbeing, *i.e.* feeling like your work makes a positive contribution to the wider world beyond the bottom line and pay cheque, but it's also a deciding factor in determining whether Millennials choose to work with a company or not as purpose and the level that a company is inspiring change lands at the front of the decision process.

According to a 2015 Deloitte Millennial survey which recorded views of 7,800 Millennials from 29 different countries, Millennials believe that companies needs to "reset" to pay as much attention to people and purpose as they do to products and profit.

In fact, 83% of Millennials believe that the success of a company should be measured in ways that extend beyond their financial performance. As such, proactivity in making a positive impact on society is a Millennial priority.

However, research suggests, rather than just having one overarching purpose statement for the entire organisation, creating team purpose statements at different levels of the organisation works better in engaging commitment from people, especially Millennials who prize purpose and meaning so much.

After all, what resonates for one team or individual may not resonate with another.

That's why research from the University of Surrey which measured commitment levels of employees suggests that, to bolster commitment, organisations should work to help individuals bolster their identity and purpose around their own teams and divisions, rather than focusing on one over-arching purpose of the organisation.

Here's how:

- Define the unique purpose of your team's existence then tie that to the wider company vision and mission. First consider the teams daily work objectives. How can these be linked to the wider purpose of the company at large? Invite each member of each team to draft team purpose statements which spell out this unique team purpose.
- Invite individuals to explore the meaning and purpose that their work gives them. Ask them to write down what excites them most about their work? What impact do they want to have on the company and the wider world? Invite them to define what their team does which no other teams within the organisation do? Ask them to write down anything they might want their team to be doing which they currently aren't and choose three to five words which summarise the team's core purpose. Once everyone has written down their answers you might ask them to share, if they feel comfortable doing so, with their colleagues to foster a sense of unity.

This kind of exercise helps foster transparency and opens up communication between individual teams and departments to help them see how they are unique and how they are united towards a common purpose too.

Transparency and Flexibility

When it comes to open communication, Millennials want plenty of it as part of an open and transparent leadership style. They've seen the corruption and mistrust that can come from a closed iron fist style of leadership. The Millennial generation wants to use the power of conversation to change the world, so they want to hear as many voices and ideas as possible.

They also favour open feedback when it comes to how they're doing, which should be continuous, like their own development. And, while they value transparent feedback, Millennials also want to be treated fairly when it comes to performance appraisals, and when it comes to diversity and inclusion and belonging.

Tenure (time in role) is less important to Millennials than performance – so they advocate rewarding people for doing a job well rather than for having done a job for a long time.

Millennials value flexibility too. They've been exposed to different ways of working and know that advances in technology enable them to work remotely from wherever there's WiFi. Work-life balance is also important to them, so they want flexibility in their working hours and adaptability in leadership style depending on individuals and circumstances.

Studies have shown that Millennials remain more loyal to companies which offer flexible working environments, rather than limiting them to stick to strict working hours or locations. But, more than that, Millennials want flexibility in their roles too. According to the Deloitte survey, they'd rather have challenging and less-structured roles with plenty of role rotation than clearly defined job descriptions or strong relationships with their immediate managers, the latter two more readily cherished by older generations.

And it makes sense that Millennials prioritise such flexibility and freedom in who they build working relationships with and how they work. After all, the Millennial generation is a connected and collaborative generation who've built an entire network of peers, compatriots and mentors with whom to work. Seeking help from a sole manager, 'the man in the corner office', is therefore of no interest to the generation who have had constant access to friends, peers and influencers online.

Support therefore comes from a multitude of mentors and peers, and that support is mutual.

What's interesting to note is the correlation between support and relationships and the way Millennials prefer to learn.

When considering the implications of this new workforce becoming the main workforce, it's important not only to consider what Millennials want but also, how they want it. For example, we know they want to grow, but how do they want to learn, so that they may progress as rapidly as they aspire to?

Insight from a Virtuali report tells us that Millennials favour experience based learning and individual learning opportunities. Their preferred learning styles tend to be coaching and mentorship, volunteerism and e-learning. They either like to learn on the job or on their own but, essentially Millennials like to learn by doing.

It's no wonder that mentorship is a favourite learning method, given that Millennials have grown up so connected to other people. Millennials have large and diverse groups of people who they interact with on a regular basis. It makes sense that other people can help them to realise their ambitions. And Millennials love to work with other people. Great news given the unprecedented level of collaboration which today's world of work demands.

This new workforce values community and committees of collaborative small teams and loves to gather and share perspectives so they may create a working environment of collective conversations about how best to achieve a shared goal.

In this way – the Millennial way – learning is mutual and global. And in this way the new majority of workers have the power to transform how we work and do business for the better.

To summarise:

How to Gain Leverage with your Millennials

- Get to know your people as individuals and invite them to participate as co-leaders in projects which see them utilising their own unique strengths.
- Create a collaborative team mindset of sharing responsibility for performance.
- Nurture the feeling of camaraderie in the workplace, because Millennials are motivated by feeling part of the team.
- Speak openly, directly and honestly and give continual feedback at individual and team level.
- Ground your motivational strategy in establishing trust, appreciation and cultivating relationships. Know each individual and what they want from work and life; how they work, where and when they work at their best.
- Regularly check that they feel that their work means something, that their skills add value to the workplace and that they feel their work has purpose, both individually and as part of a team. Show them how their work is directly impacting the company's success and the team's mission.

- Offer flexible working conditions rather than a limiting 9-5 schedule.
- Approach your diversity strategy with Millennial expectations. Research by the Institute for Public Relations (IPR) revealed that 47& of Millennials consider D&I as a determining factor in deciding where to work, compared to 37% of Baby Boomers and 33% of Generation Xers.
- Harness the tech savvy by enabling them to find shortcuts in achieving tasks and helping the business at large to do things in more efficient and productive ways. This way everyone can benefit from the Millennial way of working smarter rather than harder.
- Provide travel rewards, charity donation matching, generous maternity leave, paid volunteer work time off, birthdays off work. Brainstorm other motivating rewards with your team to give them a sense of ownership.
- Show Millennials in your workplace your bigger picture. Talk them through your roadmap and your strategy then match their own individual performance to those purposeful and strategic goals.
- Provide ample opportunities for growth; from leadership training and mentorship programmes to job-rotation projects, corporate volunteering programs and international assignments.

Chapter 8 - Mentoring, Reverse Mentoring and the Importance of Role Models

Human-capital focused initiatives are fast becoming the go-to method for getting the most out of employees and retaining top talent.

As we've explored, Millennial retention in particular is a critical issue for today's employers – not only because they are now the largest generation in the workforce and only stay in their jobs if the conditions are favourable and the opportunities satisfactory, but also because, as much as they have to learn, they have a lot they can teach older generations.

We already know that flexible environments, engaging and purposeful work and opportunities to grow and lead are favoured by Generation Y, but this generation also demands ongoing learning, preferably via coaching and mentoring support.

So, mentoring should already be on the agenda as a route to perpetual growth.

But what about inverting the hierarchy?

What about empowering Millennials to serve as mentors to their seniors?

What about opening up a two-way conduit for relevant knowledge and skills to flow between emerging and veteran leaders?

Reverse Mentoring

The concept of 'reverse mentoring' was first popularised in 1999 by Jack Welch, the former General Electric CEO. His pilot project paired 500 junior and senior staff members to enable the former to teach the latter about technological tools.

'Tipping the organisation upside down' in this way with the youngest, brightest employees teaching the oldest, has been adopted by a variety of industry leaders since those pioneering days, from Cisco to Target and beyond, each with the primary aim of "coordinating shared learning between colleagues of diverse backgrounds to create symbiotic corporate learning."

Traditional mentoring is about a wise person with many years' experience taking someone younger and less experienced under their wing. But, with the ever-changing world of enterprise advancing at breakneck speed, the tables are turning and senior leaders are now the perfect candidates to be mentored by their younger colleagues, to give them a fresher outlook and a better understanding of how the world, its talent and all its technological advances are working today.

Reverse mentoring can be based on age (Millennials mentoring older colleagues) ethnicity (BAME colleagues mentoring white colleagues) accessibility (disabled colleagues mentoring able-bodied colleagues) or sexuality (LGBTQ+ colleagues mentoring straight colleagues).

Research has shown this 'reverse mentoring' results in hugely beneficial outcomes including:

- Boosting retention of Millennials and diverse colleagues

- Gaining fresh (and refreshing) perspectives on topics which can often be missed at leadership level
- Improving clarity for senior employees about how the company is actually working on the ground
- Encouraging an environment of mutual understanding on both cultural and business issues by raising awareness about the challenges faced by diverse colleagues
- Leading cultural transformation as a result
- Challenging the hierarchy and power relationships within an organisation as junior staff members are empowered to drive the relationship
- Giving junior employees the opportunity to have their voices heard by senior colleagues
- Empowering younger staff members to affect change
- Highlighting the unique and equally valuable experiences of each individual working within an organisation and facilitating inclusivity
- Gaining and sustaining competitive advantage as a result of technological advances and heightened collaboration and innovation
- Fostering a wider sense of inclusivity and a deeper sense of belonging through better connectedness, communication and caring in a diverse world
- Developing empathy and reducing unconscious biases (more on the latter in the next chapter)
- Developing a diverse pipeline of talented leaders
- Better utilisation of internal expertise, knowledge, skills and contacts

- Keeping up with the exponential shifts in technology to stay abreast of digital advancements.

All of these are in addition to the benefits that traditional mentoring bring to a company, including:

- Encouraging and stimulating a culture of learning.
- Enabling people to gain access to different mindsets and attitudes.
- Empowering people via endorsement, sponsorship and advocacy.
- Empowering people to better understand themselves and their organisations.
- Connecting disparate knowledge to facilitate new solutions and ideas.
- Facilitating the transfer of knowledge towards more synergetic and agile teams.

Evidently, the benefits of mentoring and reverse mentoring are many.

Notably, studies have shown, not only is the retention rate of Millennial mentors increased, those senior leaders participating in reverse mentoring programmes have also gained sufficient benefits from being mentored by those younger than themselves; from gaining a deeper understanding of how to work smarter using available technology, to developing a less risk-averse and more 'possibilitarian' attitude to problems and solutions.

As such, reverse mentoring is a win-win strategy.

Digital natives (Millennials) and diverse colleagues benefit from feeling valued for their contribution and knowledge, from gaining access to senior leaders and exposure to more career opportunities, along with reassurance that their investment in the company they work for is mutually matched with investment in their own growth and development.

Digital immigrants (senior leaders) can learn a lot from digital natives to help them work more effectively and feel more comfortable in an ever-changing technological landscape.

Such facilitation of mutual knowledge-sharing from tech trends to business-oriented best practices can boost the confidence of both young and older leaders. And, as well as transferring knowledge both ways, can also assist in getting IT knowledge workers away from their tendency to work in insular silos as well.

The Learning Loop

Senior leaders have a lot to learn from their younger counterparts: from active listening, risk-taking and trend-spotting to rapid-learning, assumption-challenging and technological savvy.

They can also tap into the energy and optimism of whoever they are paired with. Take a mentor of mine, Tony Reed. He's ex-CEO of Tesco One Stop and, I'm grateful to say, he has always believed in me, given me a chance and been a real advocate for me and the direction I'm going in.

So much so that he agreed to be on our advisory board for DIAL Global. When I asked him what he's learning from me, he replied, "Your energy, bravery to put yourself out there, your resilience when knock backs occur and your courage to build a network." Meanwhile, he's taught me that hard work and resilience gets you where you need to be and that authentic inclusive leadership is the only way to lead.

Tony first started stacking shelves for Tesco aged 16 years old. Ever since then he's worked incredibly hard to become CEO for the supermarket chain he once stacked shelves for. I approached him at a networking GroceryAid event where he sat at the top table and he gave me a chance. We've stayed in touch ever since. I call him up for advice and guidance and he taps into my energy and learns from me how to get the best from my generation. We've learned from each other how to bounce back from adversity and not take no for an answer when something matters immensely.

That's the great thing about mentoring – you gain so much as a mentee and a mentor, it motivates you to want to give more, to mentor others.

In this way, great mentors inspire others to become mentors too. This pay-it-forward response where mentees are encouraged to mentor the next cohort of mentees can create a positive and highly impactful flow of inter-generational learning; one where knowledge, values and practices pass from one generation to another: a loop of perpetual learning and inspiration.

I recently sat on a panel alongside KPMG graduate Olu Odubajo who, inspired by a woman he met at a One Young World summit in Bogota, a woman who "operates movable libraries for children in war zones," decided to be proactive back in the UK in impacting change himself. Olu had read a UK Government report which showed that an increasing number of disenchanted black heritage employees were leaving their jobs to start their own businesses, only to struggle in accessing support and funding. Six months later, Olu had helped launch the KPMG Black Entrepreneurs Award after his managing partner was sufficiently impressed by a video Olu made to showcase his social mobility idea that he opted to back the concept and the awards were born.

Says Olu, "Our aim is to help black heritage entrepreneurs and their start-ups become investment ready - and accelerate, recognize and celebrate their success."

Meanwhile, as part of KPMG's Reverse Mentoring scheme, Olu mentors a UK Managing Partner on what being a black heritage colleague is like at the firm. But, as tends to be the case with all mentoring relationships, there has been a good amount of reciprocity as Olu discovered the pair has a lot of common ground. "The experience has really boosted my confidence and given me the belief that I can rise to a similar level," says Olu.

A year after meeting the woman who inspired him to make a difference, Olu returned to the One Young World Summit but, this time, he was on the rostrum himself as an ambassador, sharing his own story to 1800 attendees, "To tell them about my journey and to try to inspire others as I myself had been inspired."

This is so often what happens when people become involved in mentoring, either as mentor or as mentee – a ripple effect of reciprocal learning, growth and development which have the power to reverberate around the whole organisation.

Indeed, the benefits of reverse mentoring far exceed the reciprocal benefits for the individuals involved. They extend to the teams and the organisations in which those individuals work.

This is as a direct consequence of the collaboration and 'cross-pollination' of ideas across generations and seniority levels. By bridging the gap between diverse age-groups, genders, ethnicity and ability, this mash-up of ideas bolsters innovation and creativity, which, in turn, helps businesses to achieve and exceed desired outcomes. And, this, in turn, affects purpose, targets and profitability.

Essentially then, reverse mentoring offers a way to kill many birds with one strategic stone. The exchange of fresh ideas and new perspectives arising from such programmes fuels an array of wider possibilities envisioned, resulting in a greater chance of maintaining a strong competitive advantage.

Meanwhile, companies like Deloitte are reporting on the emergence of 'industry 4.0' and suggesting in those reports that people need to be retrained and organisations rearranged in order to 'maximise the potential value of emerging technologies.'

Reverse mentoring is one way to aid this objective.

It's also a great way to improve Diversity, Inclusion & Belonging efforts.

In Their Shoes

After all, one of the best ways to understand the challenges other people face that you don't face is to put yourself in their shoes, and the best way to do that is to mentor or be mentored by those people.

That's why KPMG chose reverse mentoring as a strategy, to help senior employees better understand the challenges those from diverse backgrounds face in the workplace. The reverse mentoring scheme pairs partners with their black heritage junior colleagues to help build a more inclusive culture.

While mentoring tends to have a focus on career progression and personal development, reverse mentoring can have other aims. In the case of KPMG, reverse mentoring is about "improving diversity and inclusion within teams, offices, and the overall firm."

The reverse mentoring scheme there has now been formalised and rolled out and, as well as providing senior leaders with insight, it's motivated junior staff to aim higher, increase their network and has given them wider exposure within the company too.

KPMG's Inclusion& Diversity Senior Lead, Edleen John, said of the reason for the scheme:

"As a firm we understand some of our diverse colleagues in the organisation don't have as much direct exposure to partners on a day to day basis. We realised there could be a disconnect between what partners think the culture in the organisation is like and what those at more junior levels are actually experiencing day to day. We wanted to work out how we can bridge that gap and create a culture of inclusion and [rather than] just running a training program, with our team saying to colleagues, 'this is what our diverse colleagues tell us', a better, more impactful way would be for them to hear directly from those colleagues in a way that will build a sustained relationship over time."

In an interview with HRD Connect, Edleen elaborated that KPMG's managing partner discovered how it might feel to be the only person of black heritage in a meeting room and how that might impact how they are able to bring their full selves to work. Until the Reverse Mentoring scheme, this wasn't something he had considered in such detail.

Generally reverse mentoring is about knowledge-sharing and reciprocal-learning, but it can have more specific drilled-down aims, such as discussing crisis points, helping each other to navigate complex decisions and enabling each other to switch roles and gain a heightened perspective about challenges faced by certain groups.

For example, Procter & Gamble's reverse mentoring programme aimed to uncover problems with accessibility by pairing disabled employees with senior leaders. The result was the discovery that internal videos were inaccessible to employees with hearing disabilities. This led to a satisfactory outcome of captions being added to all videos.

Whereas, the House of Commons ParliREACH network (the workplace equality network for Race, Ethnicity and Cultural Heritage in the Houses of Parliament) has paired members of ParliREACH with senior managers from other departments in a bid to share what it's like to work in Parliament as a member of the BAME community.

The pairings discuss challenges and have difficult diversity-led conversations with key goals being to bolster commitment among senior managers to recruit, train and promote talented people from under-represented groups and specifically BAME colleagues. The goal is also to enhance leadership, conflict management and coaching skills among pairings and educate senior managers about the challenges that BAME colleagues face inside and outside of the workplace.

The six-month scheme has led to more openness, connection and understanding about each other's perspectives, a greater mutual understanding and appreciation of each other's roles within the organisation, plus promotion for many of the participating mentors and directors.

Traditional Mentoring

To optimise learning, growth and staff retention, reverse mentoring should go hand in hand with traditional mentoring. Being taught and supported and having a sounding board to bounce ideas and issues off is a great way to learn, but cultivating these supportive relationships also helps boost wellbeing at work, as we've explored.

Primarily, though, mentoring enables us *all* to learn, grow and improve. And that's something we *all* want, whichever generation we belong to. Everyone deserves to have a mentor, or a number of different mentors, actually. I have a number of mentors myself: Leann Hearne, Sam Allen, Tony Reed, my mother, father, husband, and brother.

As Russell Brand states in his remarkable book, *Mentors*: "We, as individuals, are works in progress and through a chain of mentorship - and the collaborative evolution of systems - we can improve individually and globally, together."

In this way, mentorship can be seen as offering an aspirational pathway to growth "providing" coordinates to others who want to undertake a comparable journey", but also as something that runs in both directions.

Like Russell, we can all aim to have people we turn to "when the way ahead is not clear" as well as younger people who look to us for guidance. Opening up this two-way street is so beneficial to those who hope to lead some day and those already leading, as we have so much that we can learn from each other; so much knowledge, social capital and psychosocial support that we can provide to each other.

Reciprocity

In fact, all strong mentoring relationships tend to be about co-learning and interdependency.

Even during traditional mentoring programmes, mentoring is a two-way conduit where the mentors have learned and sufficiently grown from the experience as much as the mentee. So there is often this sense of reciprocity, co-learning and co-mentoring, where both parties learn from each other.

And, while reverse mentoring goes one step further by honing in on what the younger person can teach the older person, learning remains reciprocal and mutual.

Mentoring Methods

Mentoring comes in all shapes and sizes – from face-to-face one-to-one mentoring, to the hierarchical inversion of reverse mentoring, enabling the older generation to learn from the younger one.

Another mentoring methodology is the use of mentoring circles, which involves a number of people discussing topics and challenges, fused with elements of group coaching.

Mentor circles can also help in instances when few mentors are able to give enough time to mentor, in which case mentorship in a group setting can enable one mentor to guide multiple people and, as is often the case, peers start to mentor each other too.

Specifically set-up peer learning support, where people from the same generation support each other, is another critical mentoring method. Indeed, peer membership organisations like the one we've created with DIAL Global, where people can learn from their peers within different organisations, is a powerful way to cut down costs for pain management consultants, as peers can readily help each other out.

Another form of mentoring is distance-mentoring, where people from the same organisation but different companies mentor each other via Zoom and other virtual meeting software, or cross-company mentoring where mentoring takes place between people from different organisations.

Cross-Company Mentoring

Cross-company mentoring works well for smaller firms, or those which don't have sufficient mentors within their own senior management but have a wide range of customer organisations that could help.

The 30% club, for example, based in the UK, US and Ireland, has a cross-company mentorship scheme for mid-career level women who are keen for a mentor but not necessarily within their own firm.

This scheme is part of the club's initiative to help develop a broader pipeline of women and 'balance the pyramid' across all levels. The 30% Club state the following: "Our mentees have access to impartial advice and our mentors gain eye-opening insights into the issues being faced by women in their organisations".

Those mentored have found it liberating to develop mentoring relationships outside of their own firms, so they feel less restricted in talking about issues they face. While flagging those issues has given the mentors involved 'eye-opening insights' about what women within their own organisations face, and what might be done to rectify those issues.

Other examples of cross-company mentoring include a UK-based bank, which looked outside of its own organisation to seek mentors for its regional directors in a bid to enhance their commercial awareness. One of the bank's larger businesses was McDonald's, so senior management from the fast food chain mentored the regional managers accordingly.

Similarly, The Irish Post Office deployed a cross-company mentoring scheme to support female career advancement in junior and middle management when, short of relatable senior managers, they looked to their supply chain to help. Sometimes this kind of mentoring scheme is one way and non-reciprocal. Other times it can be run as a network of mentors across the same industry but from different companies mentoring each other.

The latter type of cross-company mentoring scheme was carried out by the UK Institute of Practitioners in Advertising where young advertising agency owners paired up with older peers. Similar schemes have been run for aspiring FDs to be mentored by members of the Institute of Chartered Accountants and aspiring HR directors by more experienced directors from the Chartered Institute of Personnel and Development. In these types of programmes, training costs can be split and perspectives can be wider.

Most of all, innovation is stimulated as mentees are exposed to different ways of doing things from those outside their own organisation.

Notably, whichever form of mentoring model a business opts to roll out, mentoring gives people what they want at work – support, regular feedback and continuous on-the-job training – so it leads to improved employee engagement, development, productivity, and retention, which means nobody loses out and everybody wins.

Role Models & Real Models

While Reverse Mentoring has its place, especially when it comes to developing empathy and reducing unconscious biases, traditionally mentors take the shape of a role model; someone we look up to, can relate to and have respect and admiration for; someone whose wisdom we will appreciate and take on board so that we may grow and progress.

With this in mind, when it comes to the Diversity, Inclusion and Belonging piece, it's critical for there to be enough role models and real models for everyone – whatever their age, gender, background, ethnicity, sexuality – to be able to relate to.

We need role and real models to emulate on our own journey and, if we're really lucky, those role models and real models we respect may advocate for us too.

That's what happened for Teresa Boughey who believes we all need cheerleaders around us to reach down and pull us up and along on their journey with them.

During our podcast conversation, Teresa told me, "Early in my career I was fortunate to have a male ambassador who really recognised the talent that I had. He was the Group HR Director for a large organisation and I worked alongside providing administrative support. However, he wanted somebody more than capable of doing his admin, someone who could progress within the field of HR. So he mentored me and would let me sit in on board meetings. So, at a young age (both professionally as well as in years), I was exposed to strategic activities, such as mergers and acquisitions and executive remuneration, all of which you don't generally gain access to unless you're on the board."

That's when Teresa learned: "The best leaders realise it's not about them having less, it's about creating more for others in the future."

Such alliances are vital for every individual but having people who really believe in you is a huge confidence booster.

And that's especially important for those who feel less likely to succeed *because* of their colour or gender or any other perceived limitation.

Feeling excluded and like you don't belong can impact on a person's self-confidence and belief in themselves. They may feel like they won't get the job or promotion, because of their race or gender or sexuality. As another podcast interviewee and D&I advocate, Susan Robson, noticed during her mentoring work with a group of BAE women.

As Susan explains, "Some people would say, "Oh well – that BAE woman is obviously going to get the job, because they tick the diversity box." Yet the BAE women felt they wouldn't get the job, precisely *because* they were BAE women".

In circumstances such as these it's absolutely critical for people who feel held back to have someone help lift them up and advocate for them; to push them forward and offer support.

Of course, sometimes we are the ones to hold ourselves back, even when we do have a strong support network.

As Olu Odubajo says, *"most of us veer between self-doubt, hope and optimism but when we realise that other people believe in us, it's up to us to start believing in ourselves."*

Certainly, we're more likely to gradually grow that self-belief and self-confidence if we have role models who are accessible, knowledgeable and who want us to succeed.

Role Models in Action – The Paul Sesay Story

When role models are accessible and they advocate for us, truly magical growth can occur. The kind of growth which leads to those who've been inspired and empowered by their role models to go on to inspire and empower others; the kind of growth which leads to purposeful work which makes a huge difference in the world, as was the case for Diverse and Inclusive Leaders podcast interviewee, Paul Sesay.

Today, Paul helps organisations on their journey to become more inclusive. His Inclusive Top 50 is a benchmark for organisations to measure themselves against, to see how inclusive they are across every strand of diversity.

After working for a number of businesses which were paying lip service to D&I, Paul found himself growing increasingly frustrated. So he set up his own business in 2006 to focus on inclusion for everyone in society, starting with a directory to help anyone who felt discriminated against, giving specific information about what to do to find work with inclusive companies.

Paul's passion for making a difference in the world was fuelled when he met his first role model and mentor. But, before then, life wasn't easy. After being fostered as a child by a wide variety of families and spending time in different institutions, *"some good, some really very bad,"* he recalls, things could have panned out very differently for Paul.

"Living with so many different families really opened my eyes to what it was like to live with different types of individuals and everything I went through made me a strong person, myself," he smiles.

Being the only black boy in his school and enduring racism from one of his foster families who, on watching Zulu, told him that his family was on TV, Paul struggled with not feeling accepted, but embraced his own black culture anyway, listening to Run DMC and reggae and cultivating his passion for music.

However, on realising at 19 that living and working on the streets in Chapeltown, Leeds was not the direction he wanted his life to go in, Paul moved to Liverpool with no clothes other than those he was wearing and £25 in his pocket.

It was there that he met a radio DJ for BBC Radio Merseyside called James Blass and that connection was to set him on the right path and change his life for the better forever.

"He took me under his wing simply because he liked me," says Paul. *"He fed me, gave me a roof over my head and showed me what it looked like to achieve your dreams; something I'd never seen before in my life."*

With no family and no one around him *"who even took note"*, James showed Paul what might be possible. That's what any good role model and mentor has the opportunity to do – to demonstrate the possibilities and guide their mentee towards seizing them.

Consequently, Paul would MC around the clubs in Liverpool and James would come to see him, calling Paul his apprentice. Says Paul, *"That was a catalyst for me to start believing in myself."*

And herein lies the power of the mentoring role model – someone to root for you; someone to not only emulate yourself but to celebrate you too.

This single role model took Paul under his wing and empowered him. As a direct result, Paul has achieved so much and has immense gratitude for that demonstration of care, connection and encouragement. It was the first time in his life he'd been shown that he had it within himself to succeed, and so he that's what he went on to do.

His first project emerged during the recession when hate crime was soaring in inner cities. Says Paul, *"I wanted to promote the role models that were keeping society going, because there was no money going into community organisations, so I started the National Diversity Awards."*

Sometimes, feeling like an outsider compels you to think outside the box and do something proactive about whatever it is that's frustrating you; to do something to prove yourself.

Businesses can tap into that proactive frustration by empowering their people to make a difference around causes that matter to them. After all, what matters to us engages us, so it's important for leaders to harness that.

Like Paul, I've always felt this constant need to prove myself. I didn't realise until I grew older that actually embracing that real, true, authentic difference is a massive positive. It acts as a driver to take positive action and that's a power which can be harnessed. And, when role models walk into our lives and offer their mentorship, that's precisely what they do – they tap into that inner frustration and drive. Mentors enable us to recognise and celebrate who we are and they empower us to do something with what we have.

Sadly James Blass passed away suddenly after battling cancer, but his funeral filled out the Anglican Cathedral, the biggest cathedral in the area, which demonstrated how much positive influence he had; *"not just in the black community,"* says Paul, *"but from everywhere, from all over the city, people came to wish him well."*

Such was the power of one mentor's influence. As Paul told me:
"James was a catalyst for me starting the National Diversity Awards. Because they are all about shining a light on role

models in society. James didn't realise how many people he'd made a difference to, so I want every nominee to know how they've inspired people, to know that they are making a difference."

In doing so, Paul hopes this will spur those role models on tenfold and encourage the younger generation to step up to inspire others too.

"If it wasn't for meeting a role model myself, who knows where I'd have ended up," ponders Paul, who was constantly invited to sell drugs when he moved to Toxteth in Liverpool.

That was when Paul recognised the importance of community organisations. Says Paul, *"There was a company which helped people in the local community get jobs. It encouraged them to get out of bed and lined up interviews for them. Meanwhile, the Charles Watton Centre in Liverpool helped people who'd failed at school to re-sit their GCSEs. They even offered £50 per week incentive to go there, which is how I got my GCSEs and went to college to study computer game production, but there's nothing like that anymore in these communities, and it's a crying shame these infrastructures of support are no longer there."*

Having been supported himself Paul felt compelled to help.

"It's not a black or Asian thing," adds Paul. *"It's a socioeconomic thing. It's the fact that many inner-city kids*

are lost and don't have the opportunities that they should have."

This has driven Paul, just as it has driven me and so many other people to want to give a voice to the underdog, to the unusual suspects; to do what we can to educate and inspire youngsters who don't have a privileged start in life; to give them the opportunities they have just as much right to as anyone else.

As a result, Paul started the Inclusive Top 50 - a benchmark of the most inclusive employers in the UK, where organisations from public to private sector across multiple industries are surveyed to gain an overview of what diversity and inclusion is like within UK society.

In establishing this initiative, Paul hopes to prevent the nonchalant box ticking of merely paying lip service to Diversity & Inclusion. Paul and the community element of his organisation digs deeper. As Paul explains, *"I look at companies' diversity policies and question, have they actually taken actions to go to the community to attract talent in all levels of their organisation? That's what inclusion is about. I want to make sure people aren't just talking about being diverse, but that they actually are diverse and inclusive."*

Paul elaborates further:
"We get to know the trends and initiatives and, as organisations are vying to be the most inclusive employer, that can only bring a lot of goodness to UK society as a whole."

So Paul's benchmark is not about telling companies what to do better, but about encouraging organisations to take action.

"Time and time again we hear organisations say, 'we find it difficult to get into communities.' So we help them to do that – to tap into the very best talent that's out there. We want organisations to look outside of the box to see actually where the talent is."

"Because community cohesion is so important; engaging in the black communities and with the ethnic groups within your local area can make a huge difference. So we put organisations in contact with the community leaders or people who are doing great stuff within that area. And we help them to build an accelerated future talent pipeline via reverse mentoring, by putting someone from a race background or LGBTQ+ background and showcasing their talent and enabling them to teach the senior leaders what they've been unaware of."

Paul also aims to connect those just starting out on their D, I& B journey with those who have already rolled-out tried and tested initiatives. *"We can connect them across sectors, so they then can share best practice between each other,"* adds Paul, whose main aim for both the National Diversity Awards and The Inclusive Top 50 is about bringing people together.

"It's all about bringing different communities which wouldn't ordinarily come together, to work together. For instance, an LGBTQ+ charity working with a Muslim charity, or a disabled charity working with a race charity. It's bringing people

together and highlighting the good work that each strand does."

In this way Paul's work is showcasing the cohesivity in diversity and tackling the issue that D&I initiatives sometimes come up against; where employee resource groups and communities are created and yet, because of that feeling of 'safety in numbers', people grouped together stick together. Whereas, being able to spread the inclusive message and share the good across community groups and provide opportunities to work cross-group with each other, that's powerful.

Coming from a loveless childhood and now having his own children, Paul sees his children as role models who inspire him to keep doing the work he's doing: *"I want them to have equal opportunities. They're mixed race and it saddens me that my son or daughter might not have the same opportunities as others, because of the colour of their skin. So that gives me inspiration to carry on doing what I'm doing."*

And Paul wouldn't be doing what he's doing if it wasn't for that first mentor, that first advocate and sponsor, that first role model guiding the way, shining a light and pulling him upwards.

More Than a Mentor – The Importance of Sponsorship

The fact is, mentors are more than just teachers. However, while they can transfer knowledge and offer professional insights, they can also make introductions, provide situational advice, offer strategic personal development and career planning, offer accountability for goal-achievement, and so on. In this way, rather than just mentor someone they can sponsor them too.

In this way, mentors in the modern and diverse workplace, should also be advocates. Especially given that research by Catalyst in Fortune 500 companies around women with MBAs and high potential have sufficient opportunities for a mentor, but not a sponsor. Why? Catalyst found that women often don't have the same access to sponsors as their male peers and that the mentoring they receive is different, and less 'strategic' than that given to men.

For example, women interviewed talked about how mentorship helped them understand themselves and their preferred operation style better, along with actions they might make to improve.

Conversely, the men interviewed talked about how mentorship gave them a routemap as their mentors helped them plan their next move and take charge in new roles, as well as endorsing their leadership potential and authority publicly.

When women are sponsored, they run with it and tend to go far. Take Leann Hearne, Group CEO of First Ark. In our DIAL

Global Fireside Chat, Leann told me her career journey from PA to CEO was, *"like most other people who had the opportunity to succeed, at the hands of other people who sponsored me."*

Certainly, when other people believe in you and advocate for you, it can have an incredibly positive impact on your career progression. *"I was really quite naïve though,"* admits Leann. *"I didn't really notice that there weren't many females in senior leadership roles until I became an MD. [Then] I realised that two or three levels below me there were equally no females, until you got down to middle manager."*

Since then, however, Leann has paid this support forward by mentoring and sponsoring others and leading by example when it comes to diversity and wellbeing in the workplace. FirstArk are strong supporters of the LGBTQ+ community and sponsor the Pride march and the company provides mental health support networks and flexible working options for staff. *"Work is not a place that you go to, it's a thing that you do,"* says Leann. *"I don't mind where it is that you do it, so long as you do [the work.]"*

Leann's career path is an example of sponsorship working well and she's been fortunate not to have experienced inequality in the sponsorship provision she's received. However, elsewhere the story is a different one.

Of course, there should be no difference in how people are mentored but, as a result of their research, Catalyst suggests that men mentoring women ought to have special training due to a tendency to "embed unconscious biases, endorse stereotypes and be blissfully unaware of the sand traps that women face in the workplace".

To really understand this issue, however, it is important to understand the difference between 'mentor' and 'sponsor'.

While mentors guide you and give you advice, sponsors will advocate on your behalf and actively try to advance your career.

But too often, women in particular will conflate the terms "mentor" and "sponsor" – often to the detriment of their careers. The Harvard Business Review went so far as to claim that "women are over-mentored and under-sponsored".

Sylvia Ann Hewlett, author of *Forget a Mentor, Find a Sponsor*, concurs with Catalyst and the Harvard Business Review and says that women often make the mistake of assuming mentors and sponsors are interchangeable. She says:

"Women on average have three times as many mentors as men -- but men have twice as many sponsors."

And, while there is a difference between mentorship and sponsorship in that mentors provide guidance as a kind of guardian angel, whereas sponsors actively advocate for your next promotion, mention you in meetings and pull you up through the organisation or, as Sylvia puts it: *"Mentors advise.*

Sponsors act." I believe mentors can sponsor you and sponsors can mentor you. There needn't be a line dividing the two.

In fact, as you get in front of your mentor more often and develop a strong relationship with them, taking their advice and guidance on board, they become more *likely* to advocate for you. They get to know you better; they get to know you've got what it takes, and this therefore enables them to advocate for you more accurately, as they know where your value is and how your potential will best be realised.

So, as well as asking if you've applied to speak at relevant conferences, your mentor/sponsor can, once they've gotten to know you via your mentorship relationship, actively recommend you to speak at relevant conferences.

What starts off as a mentoring relationship can develop into a sponsorship relationship.

Furthermore, when people suggest that sponsorship is more important than mentorship, it could have the detrimental effect of reducing the pool of eager mentors. Mentors can gradually become sponsors and, in my view, each individual deserves both from the same person.

Paul Sesay's role model was both a mentor and a sponsor without even thinking about it or meaning to be. I believe this pro-active support role is critical to help pull young leaders up.

And, most critical of all is the need for mentors, whether young or old, operating within a traditional or reverse mentoring relationship, to listen to each other and learn from each other; to believe each other and believe in each other.

Indeed, for some participants, this may be the first time anyone has ever given them support and belief in themselves.

But what else can business leaders do to get mentoring right?

How to Get Mentoring Right

- Define expectations, provide clear guidelines and goals. Decide on whether the sharing of knowledge should be informal or specific, define timescales and ensure that both mentor and mentee have clarity around what they want to get out of the relationship as a result of the scheme.
- Start small and focus on addressable issues at first, such as technology, before moving on to issues around diversity and inclusion.
- Ensure pairings are appropriately considered via surveys and/or meetings before matching mentoring pairs.
- Build trust by ensuring confidentiality.
- Remember, with reverse mentoring, it's not the reverse mentor's job to "de-bias" the senior leader they're paired with.
- Allow sufficient time for each mentorship meeting and time for each participant to write and evaluate their

own reflection reports where they consider what they're learning from each other and highlighting action steps in terms of how they might develop the role towards pro-active advocacy/sponsorship.

For when mentoring is done well and done right, the growth potential for the individuals and the company is astounding – it's a connection tool which helps participants see the world through the eyes of another which, in this increasingly diverse world, is integral to personal and business success.

CHAPTER 9 - Demystifying Diversity

"Innovation is most likely to come from parts of us that we don't all share,"
Anka Wittenberg

You might be wondering why I've left the chapter on diversity until last in a book about Diversity, Inclusion and Belonging?

One reason is that, these days, I *like* to be different.

After spending over half my life longing to be the same as everyone else, just so I might fit in with the majority, I've realised the great power in difference.

These days, I cherish my own diversity as much as I speak up about the importance of it in the workplace.

Another reason is because there is so much *more* to D&I than diversity and inclusion alone, and I wanted to explore all that there is across these pages.

As you've read, belonging is at least as important as the other factors in impacting performance, retention and wellbeing levels in the workplace, so I was keen to start the book exploring that imperative topic first.

As the book comes to a close, let's demystify what's left to demystify of the diversity piece; briefly recap on the diversity dividend and the diversity deficit and reflect on the important point that diversity is about more than race, gender and sexuality; it's about individuality, accessibility and neurodiversity too. And let's conclude with a list of actions to add to those already provided across these pages, so that you can benefit from the D, I & B opportunity and attract, engage and retain the best talent from the widest talent pool.

The Diversity Dividend and Deficit

After all, the business case for diversity is now widely accepted. Leaders now know why D&I is such an important business-critical issue. The rising percentages of polled executives saying it's important to them in Deloitte surveys tell us this, as does a recent Forbes study which revealed 85% of senior executives believe diverse, inclusive workforces are "crucial" to innovation.

Statistics on the benefits of D, I & B abound and prove that being more diverse and inclusive equals better business – from a profit, performance and growth perspective; from an innovation, brand equity and productivity perspective and from a talent attraction, engagement and retention perspective.

And it makes perfect sense given that teams of people work best as a result of difference rather than uniformity. That's as true in business as it is in sport where the best performing teams tend to have on their side the strongest kicker, the quickest runner, the highest jumper and so on. Teams of people with their own unique set of strengths, skills and perspectives, from a variety of different backgrounds, genders, ages and races work best. Obviously!

And yet, we so often throw away top talent, sometimes unintentionally, just because of the way we hire or the way we fail to engage.

As Thomas Armstrong, author of *The Power of Neurodiversity* says, "we have learned to reject a throw-away culture, yet we continue to unintentionally exclude or discard great talent."

He is talking about the 10% of people whose brains are wired differently to the majority of neurotypical people; i.e. people with dyslexia, dyspraxia, ADHD and autism.

As Andrew Pearce wisely says, "In this age of disruption, where ideas matter more than ever, having a diverse and inclusive team whose voices matter around a table garners much better results in terms of ideas and innovation."

Evidently, D, I&B is not merely a conversation for the HR department, it's all-encompassing and needs to be discussed across all levels, from ground-floor employees to C-suite and board.

It's not about compliance or 'quotas' about the golden percentage of 30%. This, as I hope we've explored fully across these pages, is not a regulatory box-ticking exercise. Giving multiple voices from multiple backgrounds the chance to be heard as they are, without hiding or covering themselves in order to fit in, but celebrating the unique and the different empowers not just the individual, but the company they work for too.

It's also not only about resource groups and labels. Grouping unique individuals together just because they share the same race or gender or sexual preference or age is not the answer either – this just leads to people feeling siloed and, although 2 can foster an increased sense of belonging among a group of people who have a lot in common, it's not the only intervention to roll out in a bid to become more diverse and inclusive.

Another reason why D, I & B is so important is because we all have unconscious biases to varying degrees. This is, as Joelle Emerson of Harvard Business Review suggests, *"not because we are bad people, but because we are people."*

Rather than be defensive about this, let's be fascinated by it and, as uncomfortable as it may feel, let's explore it and do what we can to shift our assumptions for the greater good of unity and humanity.

So, apart from unconscious bias training what can companies do?

What actions can be taken?

How can businesses think differently about difference and create company-wide inclusion which fosters a strong sense of belonging?

We've already explored a great many of the types of interventions and initiatives which business leaders can explore, but the first priority is a mindset issue.

It's about seeing diversity as more than about what's visible (race/gender/age/physical ability) but as the *cognitive* element too.

It's about seeing this diversity of thinking and inclusion of all individuals as more than a programme to be managed, but through the lens of it being mission critical.

For when we see belonging, inclusion and diversity of thinking as a business imperative, we are addressing and embracing the complexity of the world we live in.

This complexity means we each have varying ways to address problems and come up with solutions and, by giving everyone a voice at the table, we disable the risks that homogeneity can create and enable the collective power of hearing, seeing and including everyone. Like my friend and podcast guest Martin Pong says, "D&I is about having a responsibility for everyone." And that means hearing, including and catering for everyone.

In this way, businesses operating in this ever-changing world can play offence rather than defence, they can proactively shift rather than reactively carry out damage-limitation.

Doing so helps companies to access the top talent available as the talent pool becomes much wider. This, in turn, helps furnish a broader (and therefore better) leadership pipeline.

In today's transparent world, employers need to demonstrate how *any* individual can fit into their work environment.

Cultivating a culture of belonging and inclusion and employing a diverse workforce is a no-brainer if you want to be able to access and retain the best talent who'll perform at the highest level; if you want to maximise innovation and optimise customer understanding.

And, as well as tapping into the wide range of different approaches and perspectives that a diverse workforce brings with it, ensuring that different individual styles of thinking are accommodated, welcomed and encouraged will further boost connection, collaboration and creative exploration.

By now you know why D, I & B matters so much. As a counter to the problems faced in today's ever complex business landscape, you can: increase employee engagement and decrease employee turnover, improve job satisfaction and knowledge sharing, reduce workplace harassment and boardroom battles.

And, as McKinsey & Company's study of 1000 companies across 12 countries revealed, outperform on profitability (21%) and value creation (27%) as those in the top 25% for ethnic/cultural diversity were more likely to achieve above-average profitability—33% for diverse executive teams and 43% for diverse boards, whereas companies in the bottom 25% for both gender and ethnic/cultural diversity pay a penalty for a lack of diversity as they were 29% less likely to experience profitability above the industry average.

That diversity deficit demonstrates how those who are yet to wake up to the importance of D, I & B miss out on the competitive advantage gained by those who are pro-active in this space and suffer a negative impact to their business.

In fact, another McKinsey statist suggests that £24 billion is left on the shelf because companies aren't engaging certain communities.

A no-brainer then indeed!

When it comes to hiring, equality is vital. This means that employers need to put a different mixture of people into the hiring end of the funnel in order to gain a broader and more diverse workforce. You can still hire the person with the best skills and attitude and so on, but there should be a representative split of different individuals across a job search.

Having a minimum of 30% of female and diverse candidates on a long list is a start, to ensure there's an equal representation of a business community there.

Explore what the market has to offer, be pro-active about it and focus on inclusion rather than exclusion.

But, rather than focus on the traditional diversity norms, of race, of gender, of sexuality and of age, you can widen and leverage the talent pool even further by focusing on diversity of thought, because no two people think the same.

Neurodiversity

"Neurodiversity may be every bit as crucial for the human race as biodiversity is for life in general. Who can say what form of wiring will be best at any given moment?"
Harvey Blume, American Journalist in The Atlantic (1998)

Today's business climate is globalised and competitive, so we need a blend of people who think differently, who approach problems differently and who use different parts of their brains.

You can't maximise innovation and performance when you fill a room with homogenous thinkers! We need some creative 'right brained people' who have a tendency towards creativity and insight, and we need some analytical 'left brained people' who tend to be proficient in crunching numbers and data analysis.

Some people bring more emotional intelligence to their teams; others bring analytical and creative perspectives and experience.

Given that we are all wired differently, in order for our enterprises to be 'whole-brained' we need to tap into those differences, and that means being open to hiring people who don't think like we do. Rather than hire only neurotypical people, we need to hire neurodivergent colleagues too.

The fact is, human neurocognition is incredibly varied. Neurodiversity is a term used to described this sub-category of organisational diversity and inclusion which aims to support and optimise the talents of individuals who think differently, including the 10-15% of the population with autism, Asperger's, dyslexia, dyspraxia, and ADHD (attention deficit hyperactivity disorder) who, not only make up a substantial proportion of job applicants, but also customers and existing staff.

After all, we all have strengths and weaknesses in the way we think. Some of us are more creative, some of us more analytical and the strengths of neurodivergent individuals is often their capacity for problem-solving, creative insight and visual spatial thinking.

As Steve Silberman, author of *NeuroTribes*, says, "honouring and nurturing neurodiversity is civilization's best chance to thrive in an uncertain future."

A case in point is teenage climate activist and Nobel Peace prize nominee, Greta Thurnberg who has Asperger's Syndrome. She has frequently referred to her diagnosis as a gift and a superpower and a difference which has helped her see the crisis. In a post on her Facebook account the 16-year-old said that her Asperger's "means I'm sometimes a bit different from the norm. And — given the right circumstances — being different is a superpower."

In an interview with CBS, Greta said:

"It makes you think differently. And especially in such a big crisis like this one we need to think outside the box. We need to think outside our current system, [so] we need people that think outside the box and who aren't like everyone else."

Evidently, as much as it's important for action during a climate change emergency, it's important in the ever-changing world of enterprise, to tap into the talent of neurodivergent individuals.

If Greta can save the planet, imagine what someone with her style of thinking could do for your business?

Tapping the potential of neurodiverse individuals, who simply experience the world differently to varying degrees, enables them to contribute to your organisation, build a career and positively impact their lives and the lives of their colleagues.

Therefore it's of crucial importance for leaders today to recognise and invest time in understanding the common strengths and challenges shared among the neurodiverse population.

This is one of the drivers behind EY's autism hiring programme which is tapping into talent from an otherwise overlooked group of the population to fill Account Support Associate positions with people who have autism and strengths in data analysis.

Such initiatives are sorely needed as, rather alarmingly, according to the National Autistic Society, only 16% of autistic adults in the UK are in full-time employment. Yet, 77% of them want to work; while only 1% of corporate managers have dyslexia compared to a population norm of 10%.

Meanwhile, around 13,000 graduates with dyslexia join the workforce each year, so you have no doubt already hired neurodivergent individuals. But are you enabling them to thrive? We'll explore how to do this at the end of this chapter.

I was diagnosed with Dyslexia myself during my university studies. I never used to tell anyone about this, however now I feel it is a positive and I embrace this.

A friend of mine, Mamta Singhal, Commercialisation Manager for Coca Cola European Partners supply chain is an expert in the neurodiversity field and works in a predominantly male field in STEM. We were discussing our dyslexia recently and she coined the term "Dyslexiability", which went viral. It neatly summarises the fact that the strengths which dyslexics often have are valuable. In this way they can be seen as a gift.

Thankfully, many large corporations are recognising the value in the way neurodiverse talent think and perform. As such they are leading the way with neurodiversity-at-work initiatives, including Ford, Amazon, EY, Google and Microsoft to name but a few, while JP Morgan have stated 50 per cent more productivity from the autistic workers they've trained in their Mortgage Banking Technology division, and have also noted the speed in which their neurodivergent colleagues have learned what had taken neurotypical colleagues "three years to ramp up."

No wonder neurodiversity is becoming a priority in corporate agendas.

After all, inclusivity means including *everyone*, so the neurodivergent demographic should not be excluded as it previously has been.

Just as the business case for diversity suggests, doing so means missing out on top talent and the chance to bolster productivity and competitive advantage; whereas enabling a diversity of thought into your organisation and allowing those with different perspectives, experiences and background to tackle problems, develop products and analyse outcomes, results in a vastly more creative and innovative team.

Optimising Strengths and Understanding Weaknesses

Neurodiverse talent bring a wide range of valuable skills and traits into organisations.

From the capacity of ADHDers to multi-task, risk-take and remain calm under-pressure and the capacity of dyslexic and dyspraxic individuals to 'think outside the box' with their particularly strong insight, creativity, inventiveness and visual narrative thinking styles to the logical analytical thinking and problem-solving skills, focus, reliability, detailed memory retention and attention to detail often exhibited by those with autism – neurodiverse talent has a lot to offer organisations.

Thomas Jefferson and Emily Dickinson were both assumed to be autistic, as is Dan Aykroyd, Temple Grandin and Daryl Hannah. Meanwhile 10% of the population are thought to be dyslexic with famous dyslexics including Sir Richard Branson, Steven Spielberg, Da Vinci, Picasso, Warhol and Muhammad Ali. Meanwhile, Florence Welch, Daniel Radcliffe and Cara Delevingne join the 1 in 17 people who are thought to have dyspraxia. Many famous people with ADHD have channelled their energy into a talent. This is certainly true for famous chef and ADHDer, Jamie Oliver, as well as Michael Jordan, Justin Timberlake, Ryan Gosling and Adam Levine. It's also thought that Walt Disney may have had ADHD.

While it's important to consider the common strengths that neurodivergent talent brings to the table, it's also vital to consider the challenges they face if we are to help everyone to be comfortable at work and optimise their performance.

Challenges for autistic talent may include difficulty in reading social cues, providing eye contact and thinking literally or expressing feelings (even though they still feel those feelings and have EQ as much as neurotypical people). Sudden changes and over-stimulation can also discourage autistic people from working at their best.

While strong in pattern spotting, storytelling and qualitative reasoning, challenges for those with dyslexia might include trouble with working memory and processing speed, phonological processing, time management and personal organisation.

And, while people with dyspraxia can struggle with their fine or gross motor performance, hand-eye co-ordination and sensory sensitivity; they can excel at pattern-spotting, problem-solving and big-picture thinking and be incredibly resourceful.

ADHDers are often insightful, entrepreneurial, risk-taking, problem-solving, creative thinkers and, as such, highly valuable in a workplace environment. While challenges can include getting easily distracted, bored and restless if not engaged, conversely, when highly engaged in a state of flow, ADHDers tend to have a high level of focus for long durations.

However, rather than just stereotype one group of neurodiverse people as being outstanding techies and another as incredibly creative it's important to remember that no two people are alike. As Stephen Shore, autistic professor and author so rightly says, "if you've met one person with autism, you've met one person with autism."

Remember, like I said in the first chapter – leaders should be thinking about their individuals rather than their people, so it's not just about hiring neurodiverse people specifically to fit specific roles. This can work (and has done for EY) but can also be a narrow approach when, in actual fact, neurodiverse talent are individuals too and likely have a lot of unique strengths to give.

However, it's still worth knowing and considering the strengths and challenges of common neurodiverse thinking styles, even if they're not universal, in order to provide the necessary adjustments that will enable neurodiverse colleagues to thrive in the workplace.

Neurodivergent individuals, like disabled individuals, tend only to struggle when they are forced to navigate societies and workplaces which have been designed with neurotypical people in mind.

Unfortunately, this is one of the barriers people place on tapping into such talent.

Yet, such adjustments need not break the bank as they're easy to implement and low-cost.

"Rather than trying to fit square pegs into round holes, companies should create environments in which pegs of all different shapes and sizes can thrive."
Ray Coyle, CEO of Auticon

Cognitive diversity needn't be difficult. Neurodiverse talent can contribute significantly with just some simple accommodations and understanding.

The aim is to encourage and include rather than discourage and exclude job applications and hires from neurodivergent talent; to make your organisation enabling rather than disabling.

So, consider friction points and then tweak processes, work spaces and communications, which may exclude neurodiverse candidates. Assessments, tests or instructions, which rush or confuse people; job description wording which focuses on generalised role necessities, such as 'good communication skills' and making overly critical judgements based on spelling ability, work history or level of eye contact – all of these can deter neurodiverse individuals from applying for jobs and can create an unfair appraisal of them at interview stage.

Stationary work might be problematic for someone with ADHD; having to read or write lengthy reports would be challenging for someone with Dyslexia and traditional interviews might be difficult for an autistic applicant, so consideration is key.

Also consider that our work spaces and processes tend to be built with neurotypical people in mind, yet uniformity does not suit the wide spectrum of diverse human talent. Suitable adjustments to cater for everyone need not be as difficult as one might assume.

Inclusive Adjustments

Here are some ideas of workplace and process adjustments that can easily be made to cater for everyone at work, from recruitment and induction phase to enabling those with alternative thinking styles to work to the best of their abilities:

- Make job descriptions and adverts jargon-free, clear and focused on specific competencies, such as data processing ability, rather than generalised 'good communication skills'.
- Include a D, I &B statement on your website and in your job description, stating that reasonable adjustments and access requirements are happily considered. This demonstrates that your organisation welcomes cognitive diversity.
- Rather than focusing on work or educational history (where they may have not had adequate support) or spelling prowess, focus on reviewing previous work they've done or examples of times they've used their own unique strengths and capabilities.

- Consider replacing conventional interview with practical work trials or assessments.
- Adjust the interview process by providing interview questions in advance and extra time in assessments. Ask for work samples rather than psychometric tests. Provide advance information including who will be at the interview and what to expect in terms of length and format. Conduct interviews in quiet distraction-free spaces. Be specific, clear and direct.
- Give people the opportunity to disclose (or not) their neurodiversity at interview stage or at any time they feel comfortable to do so, by explaining that you have processes and adjustments in place to support them, including your proactive surveys, etc.
- Give someone in a senior leadership role the opportunity to champion and blog about neurodiversity. Doing so sends a message to existing staff as well as potential staff, customers and suppliers that you take neurodiversity seriously as advocates. Roll this out to all areas of diversity.
- Tailor inductions to individual needs to avoid overwhelming social interaction or 'ice-breakers'.
- Provide verbal or recorded instructions as well as written-ones.
- Make adjustments proactively as a result of running 'comfort-at-work' surveys.
- Tweak the working environment to enable neurodivergent employees to perform at their best and enhance their quality of working life.

- Consider providing naturally lit workspaces for employees sensitive to sensory overload.
- Provide quiet desk areas and smaller private offices to counter the noise levels of open plan environments, or simply provide earplugs or headphones. (These could be used every day or just when employees feel they need to concentrate).
- Offer desk-filing trays and 'organisation' apps for colleagues who crave personal organisation.
- Provide assistive technology, such as speech-to-text software, mind-mapping software, dictation tools, free iPad apps, dual screens and handheld organisers, along with training on how to use.
- Provide flexible working options to enable people to work from home from time-to-time or adjust working hours to help them avoid rush-hour travel.

- Carry out strengths assessments to focus on people's strengths and what they do well, rather than areas they're less capable in.
- Provide training for managers about how to respond to disclosure, sensitively introduce change and demonstrate support to neurodivergent colleagues.
- Provide mentoring for neurodiverse colleagues to act as a sounding board, to provide reassurance and support.

- Allow breaks for physical activity and a change of scene.

Some of these adjustments would be beneficial to ALL employees in helping them to do their best work, not only neurodivergent talent.

But the fact remains, simple cost-effective inclusion strategies can support neurodivergent people to live and work as neurodivergent people, rather than expect them to fit in to a neurotypical world and, in doing so, remove barriers and leverage this untapped talent pool.

The same is true when it comes to accessibility for disabled talent.

Accessibility

There are two models of disability. The medical model of disability says people are disabled by their impairments or differences. While, the social model of disability says people are disabled by the way society is organised.

According to Disability Nottinghamshire:

'Disabled people developed the social model of disability because the traditional medical model did not explain their personal experience of disability or help to develop more inclusive ways of living.'

By removing restrictive barriers, disabled people can make independent choices and have more autonomy over their lives. In this way they feel enabled rather than disabled, regardless of their medical diagnosis.

While those barriers are, thankfully, gradually, starting to be pulled down, 'disablism' still exists and those with disabilities are still frequently excluded from enjoying equal opportunities to be included at work and in society. Disabled individuals are twice as likely as able-bodied individuals to be unemployed. (48.3% of people with disabilities are in work, compared to 80.5% of non-disabled people).

As such, barriers aren't only physical, but are in the attitudes towards people with disabilities.

So how can we make our organisations more accessible to all, both in terms of removing physical and mental barriers for our disabled colleagues?

From offering audio recordings of visual print for those with visual impairments and visual productions of audio recordings for those with hearing impairments, there is more to accessibility than providing wheelchair ramps.

Firstly it's vital to let disabled talent know what they can expect from your organisation by providing an Accessibility Statement to outline what kind of support and comfort they can expect from your company.

Secondly, reverse mentoring can work particularly well when pairing disabled colleagues with able-bodied leaders in fostering deeper insight, connection and understanding from each other's perspective. Even better, some organisations are running CSR team-activities to help able-bodied and disabled teams work together in a bid to shift attitudes towards disability in the workplace.

Take Barclays, for example. Executives from the bank were paired up with disabled crew members during a Jubilee Sailing Trust expedition to form a single team pursuing a shared goal. The Jubilee Sailing Trust provides the opportunity for people of all abilities to sail tall ships on the open ocean.

All inexperienced sailors, the diverse mixture or crew members worked together to circumnavigate the coastline and resulted in a significantly positive shift in attitudes towards those with disabilities.

Interpersonal contact research has shown that when those from diverse backgrounds and social groups unite to work towards a common goal, they are more likely to develop better attitudes towards each other and form strong supportive relationships. This was true for the Barclays executives who, although were unlikely to admit having any bias about the disabled crew-members were likely to see them as different.

So those in charge of the initiative used an implicit association test (IAT) reported to "overcome social disability bias" both before and after the sailing expedition and discovered that "participants' underlying associations with disability had also significantly improved." (i.e. it wasn't just them saying their attitudes had changed, the tests proved they had.)

By universally stepping outside of their comfort zone, removing environmental barriers (thanks to full accessibility measures on board) and the requirement to work together as a team, the playing field was levelled and the stereotypes and biases held were weakened.

Evidently, the more interpersonal integration and exposure to each other leads to greater empathy, understanding and camaraderie between people who are different to each other. Only through shared experiences and teamwork can we 'discredit our negative biases' and overcome them. Such experiences allow able-bodied people to see colleagues with disabilities as individuals in their own right, rather than pigeon-holing them into one homogenous group.

How to Maximise the D, I & B Opportunity

Now that we know the positive correlation between better business performance and Diversity, Inclusion and Belonging, what can we do about it?

What practical measures can we take?

Firstly, we can demonstrate to our employees how privilege from social injustice and inequality is not always down to us –

but it is very much a reality – and, it's only by recognising it that we can work together to do something about it and make the world more socially just and equal. You may have heard of the 'Privilege Walk'. This can be a very powerful exercise to carry out with your teams.

EXERCISE: The 'Privilege Walk'

Of course everyone has some privilege to various extents. When we explore how much privilege we have, we can work towards using it for greater good, for social justice and equality. There should be no blame, shame or guilt involved in this exercise; rather the intention is for us to notice the benefits and the obstacles we each experience in life as a result of our privilege or lack of it; so we may better understand how society privileges certain individuals and not others and in which areas of our lives we do or don't have privilege.

This social justice activity ought to be carried out after trust has been fostered between participants so that open sharing can continue afterwards.

Ideally you'll need between 15 to 40 participants.

Have each person stand side-by-side in a horizontal line, all facing forward. Have a facilitator read out the following statements and invite each participant to take a step forward or backward depending on their responses.

- If your primary ethnic identity is 'White British/ American', take one step forward.
- If your first language is English, take a step forward.
- If you can publicly show affection to your romantic partner in public without fear of ridicule or violence, take one step forward.
- If your ancestors were forced to come to this country not by choice, or my necessity take one step back.
- If you were ever called names because of your race, class, ethnicity, gender, or sexual orientation, take one step back.
- If you were raised by two parents, take a step forward.
- If there were people who worked for your family as servants, gardeners, nannies, and so on, take one step forward.
- If you were ever ashamed or embarrassed of your clothes, house, car, etc. take one step back.
- If your school and work holidays coincide with religious holidays celebrated by your family, take one step forward.
- If one or both of your parents were "white collar" professionals: doctors, lawyers, take one step forward.
- If you were raised in an area where there was prostitution, drug activity, and so on, take one step back.
- If you ever tried to change your appearance, mannerisms, or behaviour to avoid being judged or ridiculed, take one step back.

- If you studied the culture of your ancestors in school, take one step forward.
- If you went to school speaking a language other than English, take one step back.
- If there were more than 50 books in your house when you grew up, take one step forward.
- If you ever had to skip a meal or were hungry because there was not enough money to buy food when you were growing up, take one step back.
- If you were taken to art galleries or plays by your parents, take one step forward.
- If one of your parents was unemployed or laid off, not by choice, take one step back.
- If you attended private school or summer camp, take one step forward.
- If your family ever had to move because they could not afford the rent, take one step back.
- If you were told that you were beautiful, smart and/or capable by your parents, take one step forward.
- If you were ever discouraged from academics or jobs because of race, class, ethnicity, gender or sexual orientation, take one step back.
- If you have ever felt unsafe walking alone at night, take one step backward.
- If anyone (other than a romantic partner) has ever made suggestive remarks to you about your body in your lifetime, take one step backward.
- If you were encouraged to attend college and/or university by your parents, take one step forward.
- If you have a disability, take one step backward.

- If you are neurodivergent, take one step backward.
- If you were raised in a single parent household, take one step back.
- If your family owned the house where you grew up, take one step forward.
- If you saw members of your race, ethnic group, gender or sexual orientation portrayed on television in degrading roles, take one step back.
- If you own a car take one step forward.
- If you were ever offered a good job because of your association with a friend or family member, take one step forward.
- If you were ever denied employment because of your race, ethnicity, gender or sexual orientation, take one step back.
- If you were paid less, treated less fairly because of race, ethnicity, gender or sexual orientation, take one step back.
- If you were ever accused of cheating or lying because of your race, ethnicity, gender, or sexual orientation, take one step back.
- If you ever inherited money or property, take one step forward.
- If you had to rely primarily on public transportation, take one step back.
- If you were ever stopped or questioned by the police because of your race, ethnicity, gender or sexual orientation, take one step back.

- If you were ever afraid of violence because of your race, ethnicity, gender or sexual orientation, take one step back.
- If your parents own their own business, take one step forward.
- If you were generally able to avoid places that were dangerous, take one step forward.
- If you were ever uncomfortable about a joke related to your race, ethnicity, gender or sexual orientation but felt unsafe to confront the situation, take one step back.
- If you were ever the victim of violence related to your race, ethnicity, gender or sexual orientation, take one step back.
- If your parents did not grow up in the UK, take one step back.
- If your parents attended college or university take one step forward.
- If your parents told you that you could be anything you wanted to be, take one step forward.
- If you are able to take a step forward or backward, take two steps forward.
- If you are a white male, take one step forward.

Once all the statements have been read out and all participants have moved backward or forward for each, look at where everyone is stood and open up discussion.

Invite participants to discuss how this activity has made them feel? Is it enlightening and eye opening or uncomfortable?

Does it divide us or bring us together? The aim is for the latter - to make us see that none of our answers to these questions are our fault - society has created privilege and lack of it, so it is up to us to figure out ways to create a more level playing field for the generations that follow.

Discuss ways we can do this, together.

In addition to the various exercises and suggestions peppered throughout the pages of this book, here are some additional actions business leaders can take to optimise the D, I & B opportunity for their organisations.

- **Ensure diverse representation is communicated across all marketing channels.** Your website imagery and job descriptions should feature a diverse mix of individuals to demonstrate that your teams are equipped with a diverse range of talent and that all individuals are welcomed, included and valued. Ultimately, images should represent your organisation's diverse culture and be consistent with your diversity policy.
- **Clearly articulate and communicate your D, I & B policy internally too.** Publish it online, across intranets and in PR material, in job adverts and via internal e-newsletters. Your policy is your promise. So make sure your staff are aware of what your policy is and fully understand it.
- **Set clear boundaries at recruitment stage**. At interview stage, specify a zero tolerance for conscious

gender, racial and sexual orientation bias and explain what initiatives you have in place to enable staff to work through unconscious bias. Demonstrating utmost clarity around these boundaries at recruitment stage helps limit possible issues and reassures potential staff members they'd be joining a trusted and safe culture, should they be offered a position at your firm.

- **Assess talent pipeline metrics.** How many diverse candidates are applying, being offered positions and accepting positions? Look for gaps to try to fill. If there's a high percentage of diverse candidates attending interview but not many being hired, could there be bias during the interview process. Or, if there's a lack of diverse candidates accepting offers or applying for roles, your branding may not suggest you are diverse enough. Remember, applicants do their homework and consider diversity as a key criteria nowadays.
- **Monitor progression of diverse talent through the organisation.** Are diverse colleagues being promoted, rewarded, included? How so? If not, what initiatives from this book could you implement to change that?
- **Explore the end-to-end employee experience.** Is every single individual truly enabled and free to bring their best selves to work and in order to foster inclusivity and belonging on a daily basis?
- **Ask consistently.** Regularly ask employees how you're doing and what you could be doing better to help them feel comfortable, engaged and valued. How can you make them feel known, understood and valued as

individuals? Are they included in making decisions? How does that make them feel? Remember the importance of how you make your people feel at work.

- **Provide unconscious bias training workshops for all staff to raise awareness and inspire change.** Explore what unconscious bias is, how it affects people who are biased against and what reinforces it? Invite employees to consider and assess their own personal assumptions and potential biases when it comes to working in teams, recruitment, promotion, and so on, so they can learn to shift their assumptions and biased behaviour accordingly

- **Offer further optional diversity training.** Explore the concepts of covering and belonging and the different variations of diversity, including neurodiversity and discuss ways to make each other feel more comfortable, accepted and valued in the workplace.

- **Keep track of and acknowledge multi-cultural religious holidays.** Enable flexibility for those who may need to adapt their schedules to fit with their culture's holiday celebrations.

- **Assess team diversity and mix it up.** Look at which teams are homogenous and see how you might make the team more diverse.

- **Demonstrate how much you value individuals by rewarding fairly.** Ensure pay equality, annual bonus equality, and recognition and reward equality.

- **Measure the impact of new initiatives.** Design ways to assess your initiatives and track progress, so you can roll out the most effective ones.

- **Give Employee Resource Groups a Voice to empower underrepresented groups.** If you are going to use employee resource groups where women, people of colour, LGBT, Millennials or neurodivergent colleagues form groups to share experiences, ensure that individual voices are heard and that a focus on individuality as well as group voices are given the opportunity to voice opinions, lead initiatives, join talent pipeline development and track their impact.
- **Establish mentoring, sponsorship and reverse mentoring schemes**. These will provide all colleagues with a chance to be heard; provide people from different backgrounds to gain alternative perspectives, increase empathy and enable all diverse colleagues to be visible and achieve their full potential.
- **Ensure balance in the boardroom as well as the office.** Get a diverse mix of people onto the board because, as much as you *say* you're big on D, I & B, if your board consists predominantly of grey-haired white-skinned men, the people you hire will not be able to see themselves growing with your company.
- **Select people who think differently for leadership development.** The wider the variety of perspectives across leadership and within teams, the better. Especially consider neurodiverse colleagues with ADHD and other neurominorities who can, in general, have a tendency toward embracing uncertainty and managing change well as a result.

Conclusion – Make Those Changes & Get In Shape

"Living in new shapes, reshapes our thinking,"
Lois Farfel Stark

Change starts from within.

The problem is that we are shaped by external influences (social, historical, political, cultural, personal practices, experiences and expectations).

This means our perspectives and world-views, our ways of habitually behaving and relating become 'shapes' which shape who we are and how we perceive ourselves the world we inhabit, and we can't shift those 'shapes' until we open up to allow them to be reshaped, remoulded and shape the change we want to be (and see) in the world.

That part is within our control, as is how we treat others and relate to them; how we make people feel with our own behaviour and actions. Of course, not everything is within our control. But, part of being a good Leader is to embrace that uncertainty and lead anyway.

I never set out to become an entrepreneur. I was certain, with my First Class Honours degree; the highest mark in my graduating year, I'd be snapped up by one of the graduate programmes I applied for (and I applied for them all). My grades got me through the door with all the big corporations but not being offered a role led me to start my own businesses.

Fast forward to present day and I get to speak out on issues around Diversity, Inclusion and Belonging and lead great teams through changing for the better. So I'm grateful for the, albeit uncertain, path I've been on, and all the lessons I've learned en route.

Life is a labyrinth. You never know which way its twists and turns will take you next... however an open mind results in an open heart and sometimes it's ok not to know what's around the corner.

This book honours those I have encountered along life's fortuitous path in both business and in life, as well as the people and businesses that have inspired me to keep going when times have been tough. It recalls some of the insights and pearls of wisdom I have gleaned from many individuals who have spoken words that have resonated with me and that I hope resonate with you too.

Regardless of being right for business in terms of profitability, influence and impact; fostering diversity, inclusion and belonging at work is the right thing to do for humanity.

My wish is that, on your own leadership journey, you will invite and welcome people in to your organisation and, in doing so, unleash the breadth of human potential. That's what good leadership is all about. Rather than focusing entirely on being the best ourselves, it's about making everyone else better and making everyone else feel like they matter.

Because, together we rise.

As Leena Nair, Chief Human Resources Officer (CHRO) of Unilever says,

"Learn without inhibitions. Be curious about things and you will find your purpose. Know that your voice matters. Know you have it in you to make a difference."

I hope this book offers a window through which we can peer together through the eyes of others, so we may consider how we can all be a force of change to move the dial in the right direction.

Because anyone can be a leader and can make a positive difference in both business and in life.

The question is: what type of leader will **you** be?

CHAPTER-BY-CHAPTER SUMMARY

INTRODUCTION

What do people and organisations really need in order to thrive? To feel connected, humans need to feel seen, heard and valued. Conversely, when our voices aren't heard, our whole selves aren't seen and our ideas aren't valued, we feel disconnected. We feel disengaged. We feel like we don't belong.

Given the alarming statistics around employee disengagement and the fact that belonging - a core essence of our being - motivates us to do well, business leaders can help everyone they hire to optimally function if they create workplace cultures which give people the gift of feeling like they truly belong.

Additionally, leaders who listen can help individuals feel included. Belonging and inclusion are intrinsically linked because they honour and empower each valuable voice. And, when that happens, each person is more likely to perform to the best of their ability, which is as good for business as it is for humanity. The right kind of workforce is one where every single individual within it is able to bring their true and whole selves to work and, rather than changing who they are in order to fit in, feel empowered to be themselves, be different and be welcomed, valued and included. Because difference is good.

Difference is so good, in fact, it's what businesses need! To stand out from the competition, to gain competitive advantage, enterprises need a Unique Selling Point, so they need difference. By tapping into a broad range of different cultural backgrounds, ethnicities, genders, sexualities and thinking styles across the whole spectrum of what the wonderful human race has to offer, business, the economy and humanity benefits.

CHAPTER 1 - Inclusion and Belonging – The Keys to Unlocking a Diverse Workforce

Over three decades, D&I has evolved. So much so, it might now perhaps be referred to as D, I & B – Diversity, Inclusion & Belonging. Especially since statistics are showing that simply having a diverse workforce, is not enough.

Representation, contribution and a celebration of difference is required. Belonging is the missing part of the D&I equation which, when the power of each are harnessed together equates to maximum employee engagement. And, not only that, the more people belong, feel included and psychologically safe, the more likely they are to stay.

Diversity is about representing a diverse mix of different people. Inclusion is about connection, participation and encouragement; how well you enable your people to mix. Belonging is enabling your people to bring their unique and authentic selves into that mix. It's about feeling seen, heard and accepted as we are, without having to change in order to 'fit in'.

So D, I &B is about a duality between similarity (having role models who have something in common with us, who we feel a sense of connection and kinship with) and difference (having our uniqueness valued and included). In this way, it's about individuals as well as tribes. Hence the importance of shining a light on similarities and differences, so we may cultivate and celebrate both.

CHAPTER 2 - The Whole Self and the Importance of Authenticity

Authenticity is crucial, not only when it comes to belonging, but also when it comes to connection. It's harder to get to know you if you're not really being you at all.

When we hire people, we don't ask them to leave part of themselves at home. We want them to show up as themselves, their best selves, their whole selves. And yet, the pressures society puts on everyone to conform, along with the internal corporate pressure to fit in, can lead the people we've gone to the trouble of interviewing and shortlisting and hiring and training to only partially show up.

According to research by the Centre for Talent Innovation, 37% of African-Americans and Hispanics and 45% of Asians say they "need to compromise their authenticity" to conform to their company's standards of demeanour or style. Meanwhile there has been sufficient research on women in STEM to suggest that acting "like a man" can be advantageous in becoming a leader in these fields. We fear being excluded and marginalised; fear of standing out for being different and the consequential fear of being affiliated with a minority group.

And when our energy is expended on masking parts of our personality, that energy is not directed to doing our jobs. In this way masking our true and whole selves is costly for the businesses we work for.

This pressure to conform and the consequential "covering" is causing D&I efforts to stall. So what can we do about it? We can discover and uncover the extent of covering in our own organisations by carrying out surveys and having discussions about it. And we can assess these issues and come up with an 'authenticity in action' plan to rectify the need to cover.

CHAPTER 3 - How to Lead Well

People who show up authentically inspire more and connect better. Consequently, when leaders share their own stories of 'uncovering', it eases the process of uncovering for everyone else. It removes the pressure and enables staff to relate on a deeper human level to the people they work for and with.

That's how leaders can lead by example to build trust, cultivate connection and develop empathy. This fosters a 'we're in this together' mentality and an open-communicative culture. This united vibe can instantly put people at ease and make them feel more comfortable about sharing what would usually feel uncomfortable.

It may feel difficult to step up to the parapet. Leadership and vulnerability may seem like strange bedfellows but, conversely, when we remove our armour, we remove our fear. Opening up helps others become more open to you, respectful of you and trusting in you.

Talking about how exclusion feels and what it's like to feel different or like an imposter or like you have to conform enables self-growth and, when others become their whole selves at work as a result of this openness, the business grows too.

CHAPTER 4 - Emotional Intelligence and Maturity

Today, strong leadership requires more than IQ, it also requires EQ and EM (Emotional Intelligence and Emotional Maturity). Today, to lead well, you need to be able to identify, understand and manage your own emotions and grasp how they relate to other people. But, even more than that, to really get to know, understand and empathise with each individual in your charge and to lead with service, as well as Emotional Intelligence (EQ) you need Emotional Maturity (EM) too.

If you can suspend self-interest in favour of the success of others, you bring Emotional Maturity to the table. Equally, when you share your own vulnerabilities, despite it feeling outside of your comfort zone; when you focus on developing cultural competencies and building trust, despite the office politics and hierarchal systems around you, it's possible to demonstrate an Emotional Maturity which will serve you and those you work with.

Through active listening and story sharing and by bringing the five pillars of Emotional Intelligence to the table – self-awareness, self-regulation, motivation, social skills and empathy, leaders can better understand themselves and others and, in doing so, help their people "get where they would've have got by themselves."

CHAPTER 5 - Purposeful Culture and Leadership

Behavioural science shows that, as humans, we all have a basic need to contribute to something bigger than ourselves. Purpose fulfils this need. Both our own inner purpose and that of the companies we work for. And if the two are aligned – that's a powerful match, which brings out the best in people and enables companies and their people to flourish.

Ultimately, human beings need meaning – that sense that our life has inherent value and significance, based on what we do and why we do it. When we go to work we need something to believe in and work towards that runs deeper than making money.

A strong purpose inspires and motivates, satisfies and clarifies. It feeds strategy, branding and engagement, both of customers and employees. It explains why you are pursuing your goals and is reflected in how you create and sell your products and services. In achieving all of this, purpose outlives every campaign, strategy and project. It's the golden thread which runs through it all.

The bottom line is, companies which have a clear purpose outperform those which don't – they generate more revenue, attract and retain more talent, keep that talent engaged and have more loyal customers. They also both manage change and innovate better.
So what do you need to do to embed purpose into a business? This chapter explores this question and provides the answers; from authentic servant leadership and a product or service which solves problems and make a positive impact to planning with the focal purpose in mind and purposeful recruitment.

Ultimately, when you hire purpose-led individuals to work for you, you create a perpetual energy and motivation which gives everyone a sense of meaning. And, as showcased in this chapter, leaders who lead with their own strong sense of 'why' inspire others to work for something beyond themselves.

CHAPTER 6 - Wellbeing – Cultivating a Happy and Engaged Workforce

Everyone deserves to be happy at work given we spend most of our time and lives there. And a happy workforce equates to a productive one. The more people feel happy and supported in their roles, the more likely they are to stay with a company. So how do we enable people to thrive, contribute and flourish at work? Rather than get people from stressed out and overwhelmed to normal, we can get them from normal to optimal functionality where they are happy and productive by adhering to the six 'pillars' of wellbeing (PERMA-V). These are: Positive Emotion, Engagement, Relationships, Meaning, Achievement, and Vitality.

Leaders can encourage positive talk about progress, strengths and outcomes, instil gratitude, encourage kindness, record instances of inspiration and help colleagues to build psychological capital. They can ensure that the working environment is positive and engaging, enable employees to find flow by getting absorbed in tasks which engage them, and ensure individuals are well rewarded and appreciated.

Meanwhile, supportive relationships can be cultivated, connections deepened and virtual boardrooms created. Purpose can be established, encouraged and pursued, ideas can be nourished and achievements can be celebrated. There's so much leaders can do to foster and bolster a high level of workplace wellbeing. And when they do, everyone benefits, as does the business itself.

CHAPTER 7 – The Millennial Way

With many already in their 30s, the Millennial Generation are already the largest workforce demographic in the US (35%) and are set to make up 75% of the entire workforce by 2025, changing the composition of our modern workplace and leadership forever.

The impact of Millennials assuming leadership roles is noteworthy because they won't stay in a job where they feel undervalued or marginalised. This listening and questioning generation is mobile and flexible and wants to do work which is meaningful, so it's critical for enterprises today to accommodate this generation.

The Millennial generation has grown up in a world where corporations and their leaders have been reported to be up to no good; where fake news has proliferated and led to an array of political and corporate storms, and in an economy which saw their parents and older peers enduring a recession and, in many cases, losing their jobs as a result. These circumstances have created a generation of people who are self-starters; keen to build and create; a generation with little trust in traditional hierarchal leadership and one which questions and examines to find the truth, rather than blindly accept it; a gift for organisations which value innovation and risk-taking.

Evidently there is much to gain from the openness and diversity-led perspective the Millennial Generation has much to offer.

They want to lead. But what else do they want? This chapter serves to answer this question, so organisations can embrace the Millennial ideal of leadership; provide sufficient opportunities for growth and ample flexibility, transparency and purpose-lead projects for Millennials to get their teeth into.

CHAPTER 8 – Mentoring, Reverse Mentoring and the Importance of Role Models

Mentoring is a powerful way for people to learn from their peers, their seniors and also, with the rise in reverse mentoring, from their juniors and people who are different from themselves.

Inverting the hierarchy by empowering Millennials to serve as mentors to their seniors has fast become a great method of opening up a two-way conduit for relevant knowledge and skills to flow between emerging and veteran leaders. The concept of 'reverse mentoring' was first popularised in 1999 by Jack Welch, the former General Electric CEO when he paired 500 junior and senior staff members to enable the former to teach the latter about technological tools.

But reverse mentoring isn't just based on age (Millennials mentoring older colleagues), it can also be based on ethnicity (BAME colleagues mentoring white colleagues) accessibility (disabled colleagues mentoring able-bodied colleagues) or sexuality (LGBTQ+ colleagues mentoring straight colleagues).

As well as boosting talent retention, reverse mentoring helps diverse colleagues to affect change, increases empathy and clarity and reduces unconscious bias and perspectives, which can be missed at leadership level. Plus, it's great way to improve Diversity, Inclusion & Belonging efforts. After all, one of the best ways to understand the challenges other people face that you don't face is to put yourself in their shoes, and the best way to do that is to mentor or be mentored by those people.

In addition to reverse mentoring, this chapter explores traditional mentoring, sponsorship and cross-company mentoring. Another benefit of mentoring is the provision of role models. As Founder and Director of The National Diversity Awards, Paul Sesay explains in this chapter, the power of role models should never be overlooked in offering those with potential a greater belief in being able to achieve it.

CHAPTER 9 - Demystifying Diversity

There is so much *more* to D&I than diversity and inclusion alone. Belonging is vital, but so are the various parts of diversity.
Diversity is about more than race, gender and sexuality; it's about individuality, accessibility and neurodiversity too.
So this chapter demystifies what's left to demystify of diversity, outlines the diversity dividend and deficit and provides a list of actions to help leaders truly benefit from the D, I & B opportunity and attract, engage and retain the best talent from the widest talent pool.
Because as much as we group people together in employee resource groups, and there are benefits to doing so, it's crucially important to recognise that no two people think the same. Leaders can embrace that and, one way to demonstrate

this is by exploring the importance of neurodiversity and how neurodiverse talent, including those who think differently as a result of having ADHD, Asperger's, Autism, Dyslexia or Dyspraxia, can bring a wealth of expertise, creativity, analytical ability and a diverse range of skills and thought processes to our organisations.

What can we do to welcome and include neurominorities to work in our enterprises? This chapter explores the range of inclusive adjustments we can carry out to make their working lives as comfortable as possible, and the practical measures we can take to make the most of the D, I & B opportunity going forward.

Conclusion: Make Those Changes and Get In Shape

Change starts from within. But external influences can shape our thinking. So, we need to open up to different ways of thinking in order to reshape those 'shapes'; to get in better shape so we can be more inclusive, less bias, more welcoming of diverse talent and less set in our ways.

When we do this we can empower the breadth of human potential. That's what good leadership is all about. Rather than focusing entirely on being the best ourselves, it's about making everyone else better and making everyone else feel like they matter.

ABOUT THE AUTHOR

Leila McKenzie Delis

Leila is a passionate thought leader with multiple business and charitable interests. She spends her time dedicated to managing numerous Directorships, advisory and committee positions whilst continuing to promote and campaign for the benefits of Diversity, Inclusion and Belonging in business & in wider society.

Leila was born in Hong Kong and holds a 1st Class Honours Degree in International Business and Business and Management Studies from highly regarded British Universities. She was awarded the RWR Award for the highest performing student in her graduating year. Leila had a uniquely entrepreneurial career since graduation, including working on multiple contract assignments with events management and corporate marketing and promotional assignments for businesses such as Nestle, Coca Cola and Unilever. She also founded and opened her own tearoom restaurant in York prior to working in Executive Search for several privately-owned organisation's before establishing her own businesses.

Leila has been proactive in her external engagements & has spoken at "Women in Sustainability" & the highly publicised Diversity Dividend Conference where she was interviewed by the journalist, Clive Myrie. She personally hosts high-profile and well-established executive and charitable events such as "Celebrating Diverse & Inclusive Leadership" & "Women in Leadership" with inspirational thought leaders from industry.

Leila also hosts a weekly podcast called "Diverse & Inclusive Leaders" on Apple podcasts and other leading podcast apps, in addition to hosting interviews with thought leaders on the DIAL Global YouTube channel.

You can find out more about Leila and her businesses by visiting:

www.leilamckenzie.com (/podcast)

www.dialglobal.org (/podcast)

You can also follow Leila on LinkedIn, Twitter, Facebook or Instagram or get in touch with her or one of her team using the contact information on the following page.

Leila McKenzie Associates

www.leilamckenzie.com

Leila McKenzie Associates is a bespoke Executive Search & Services firm operating both nationally and internationally. Leila has a proven track record of recruiting Senior Management to Board level and C-suite level positions throughout the UK and Internationally. Passion, tenacity and personal service is at the heart of all the work carried out & each individual search mandate is managed personally by Leila with the backing of a highly skilled and dedicated research function; ensuring that consistency, personal service and continuity are achieved & that each assignment is nurtured to a successful conclusion.

Get in touch with Leila and her team at:

leila@leilamckenzie.com

enquiries@leilamckenzie.com#

DIAL Global

www.dialglobal.org

Leila is also CEO of DIAL Global (Diverse, Inclusive, Aspirational Leaders) an online and "in person" community.

The purpose of the organisation is to further develop diversity, inclusion and belonging within business and wider society by giving leaders the knowledge and network to foster sustainable & positive change.

DIAL Global specialises in digital and executive education with a focus on peer to peer learning and offers a programme of innovation workshops and exclusive events lead by the world's most innovative companies.

Get in touch with Leila and her team at:

leila@dialglobal.org

hello@dialglobal.org

Index